COLLECTED WORKS OF HENRY LOUIS MENCKEN

D1829192

Copyright © 2007 BiblioBazaar
All rights reserved
ISBN: 978-1-4346-4214-1

Collected Works of Henry Louis Mencken

Damn!
and
In Defense of Women

BIBLIOBAZAAR

Collected Works of Henry Louis Mencken

CONTENTS

DAMN!
A BOOK OF CALUMNY

IN DEFENSE OF WOMEN

DAMN!

A BOOK OF CALUMNY

I.
PATER PATRIÆ

If George Washington were alive today, what a shining mark he would be for the whole camorra of uplifters, forward-lookers and professional patriots! He was the Rockefeller of his time, the richest man in the United States, a promoter of stock companies, a land-grabber, an exploiter of mines and timber. He was a bitter opponent of foreign alliances, and denounced their evils in harsh, specific terms. He had a liking for all forthright and pugnacious men, and a contempt for lawyers, schoolmasters and all other such obscurantists. He was not pious. He drank whisky whenever he felt chilly, and kept a jug of it handy. He knew far more profanity than Scripture, and used and enjoyed it more. He had no belief in the infallible wisdom of the common people, but regarded them as inflammatory dolts, and tried to save the republic from them. He advocated no sure cure for all the sorrows of the world, and doubted that such a panacea existed. He took no interest in the private morals of his neighbors.

Inhabiting These States today, George would be ineligible for any office of honor or profit. The Senate would never dare confirm him; the President would not think of nominating him. He would be on trial in all the yellow journals for belonging to the Invisible Government, the Hell Hounds of Plutocracy, the Money Power, the Interests. The Sherman Act would have him in its toils; he would be under indictment by every grand jury south of the Potomac; the triumphant prohibitionists of his native state would be denouncing him (he had a still at Mount Vernon) as a debaucher of youth, a recruiting officer for insane asylums, a poisoner of the home. The suffragettes would be on his trail, with sentinels posted all along the Accotink road. The initiators and referendors would be bawling for his blood. The young college men of the *Nation* and the *New Republic* would be lecturing him weekly. He would be used to scare children in Kansas and Arkansas. The chautauquas would shiver whenever his name was mentioned . . .

And what a chance there would be for that ambitious young district attorney who thought to shadow him on his peregrinations—and grab him under the Mann Act!

II
THE REWARD OF THE ARTIST

A man labors and fumes for a whole year to write a symphony in G minor. He puts enormous diligence into it, and much talent, and maybe no little downright genius. It draws his blood and wrings his soul. He dies in it that he may live again . . . Nevertheless, its final value, in the open market of the world, is a great deal less than that of a fur overcoat, half a Rolls-Royce automobile, or a handful of authentic hair from the whiskers of Henry Wadsworth Longfellow.

III
THE HEROIC CONSIDERED

For humility and poverty, in themselves, the world has little liking and less respect. In the folk-lore of all races, despite the sentimentalization of abasement for dramatic effect, it is always power and grandeur that count in the end. The whole point of the story of Cinderella, the most widely and constantly charming of all stories, is that the Fairy Prince lifts Cinderella above her cruel sisters and stepmother, and so enables her to lord it over them. The same idea underlies practically all other folk-stories: the essence of each of them is to be found in the ultimate triumph and exaltation of its protagonist. And of the real men and women of history, the most venerated and envied are those whose early humiliations were but preludes to terminal glories; for example, Lincoln, Whittington, Franklin, Columbus, Demosthenes, Frederick the Great, Catherine, Mary of Magdala, Moses. Even the Man of Sorrows, cradled in a manger and done to death between two thieves, is seen, as we part from Him at last, in a situation of stupendous magnificence, with infinite power in His hands. Even the Beatitudes, in the midst of their eloquent counselling of renunciation, give it unimaginable splendor as its reward. The meek shall inherit—what? The whole earth! And the poor in spirit? They shall sit upon the right hand of God! . . .

IV
THE BURDEN OF HUMOR

What is the origin of the prejudice against humor? Why is it so dangerous, if you would keep the public confidence, to make the public laugh? Is it because humor and sound sense are essentially antagonistic? Has humanity found by experience that the man who sees the fun of life is unfitted to deal sanely with its problems? I think not. No man had more of the comic spirit in him than William Shakespeare, and yet his serious reflections, by the sheer force of their sublime obviousness, have pushed their way into the race's arsenal of immortal platitudes. So, too, with Aesop, and with Balzac, and with Dickens, to come down the scale. All of these men were fundamentally humorists, and yet all of them achieved what the race has come to accept as a penetrating sagacity. Contrariwise, many a haloed pundit has had his occasional guffaw. Lincoln, had there been no Civil War, might have survived in history chiefly as the father of the American smutty story—the only original art-form that America has yet contributed to literature. Huxley, had he not been the greatest intellectual duellist of his age, might have been its greatest satirist. Bismarck, pursuing the gruesome trade of politics, concealed the devastating wit of a Molière; his surviving epigrams are truly stupendous. And Beethoven, after soaring to the heights of tragedy in the first movement of the Fifth Symphony, turned to the sardonic bull-fiddling of the *scherzo*.

No, there is not the slightest disharmony between sense and nonsense, humor and respectability, despite the skittish tendency to assume that there is. But, why, then, that widespread error? What actual fact of life lies behind it, giving it a specious appearance of reasonableness? None other, I am convinced, than the fact that the average man is far too stupid to make a joke. He may *see* a joke and *love* a joke, particularly when it floors and flabbergasts some person he dislikes, but the only way he can himself take part in the priming and pointing of a new one is by acting as its target. In brief, his personal contact with humor tends to fill him with an accumulated sense of disadvantage, of pricked complacency, of sudden and crushing defeat; and so, by an easy psychological process, he is led into the idea that the thing itself is incompatible with true dignity of character and intellect. Hence his deep suspicion of jokers, however adept their thrusts. "What a damned fool!"—this same half-pitying tribute he pays to wit and butt alike. He cannot separate the virtuoso of comedy from his general concept of comedy itself, and that concept is inextricably mingled with memories of foul ambuscades and mortifying hurts. And so it is not often that he is willing to admit any wisdom in a humorist, or to condone frivolity in a sage.

V
THE SAVING GRACE

Let us not burn the universities—yet. After all, the damage they do might be worse . . . Suppose Oxford had snared and disemboweled Shakespeare! Suppose Harvard had set its stamp upon Mark Twain!

VI
MORAL INDIGNATION

The loud, preposterous moral crusades that so endlessly rock the republic—against the rum demon, against Sunday baseball, against Sunday moving-pictures, against dancing, against fornication, against the cigarette, against all things sinful and charming—these astounding Methodist jehads offer fat clinical material to the student of mobocracy. In the long run, nearly all of them must succeed, for the mob is eternally virtuous, and the only thing necessary to get it in favor of some new and super-oppressive law is to convince it that that law will be distasteful to the minority that it envies and hates. The poor numskull who is so horribly harrowed by Puritan pulpit-thumpers that he can't go to a ball game on Sunday afternoon without dreaming of hell and the devil all Sunday night is naturally envious of the fellow who can, and being envious of him, he hates him and is eager to destroy his offensive happiness. The farmer who works 18 hours a day and never gets a day off is envious of his farmhand who goes to the crossroads and barrels up on Saturday afternoon; hence the virulence of prohibition among the peasantry. The hard-working householder who, on some bitter evening, glances over the *Saturday Evening Post* for a square and honest look at his wife is envious of those gaudy drummers who go gallivanting about the country with scarlet girls; hence the Mann act. If these deviltries were equally open to all men, and all men were equally capable of appreciating them, their unpopularity would tend to wither.

I often think, indeed, that the prohibitionist tub-thumpers make a tactical mistake in dwelling too much upon the evils and horrors of alcohol, and not enough upon its delights. A few enlarged photographs of first-class bar-rooms, showing the rows of well-fed, well-dressed *bibuli* happily moored to the brass rails, their noses in fragrant mint and hops and their hands reaching out for free rations of olives, pretzels, cloves, pumpernickle, Bismarck herring, anchovies, *schwartenmagen*, wieners,

Smithfield ham and dill pickles—such a gallery of contentment would probably do far more execution among the dismal *shudra* than all the current portraits of drunkards' livers. To vote for prohibition in the face of the liver portraits means to vote for the good of the other fellow, for even the oldest bibulomaniac always thinks that he himself will escape. This is an act of altruism almost impossible to the mob-man, whose selfishness is but little corrupted by the imagination that shows itself in his betters. His most austere renunciations represent no more than a matching of the joys of indulgence against the pains of hell; religion, to him, is little more than synthesized fear . . . I venture that many a vote for prohibition comes from gentlemen who look longingly through swinging doors—and pass on in propitiation of Satan and their alert consorts, the lake of brimstone and the corrective broomstick . . .

VII
STABLE-NAMES

Why doesn't some patient drudge of a *privat dozent* compile a dictionary of the stable-names of the great? All show dogs and race horses, as everyone knows, have stable-names. On the list of entries a fast mare may appear as Czarina Ogla Fedorovna, but in the stable she is not that at all, nor even Czarina or Olga, but maybe Lil or Jennie. And a prize bulldog, Champion Zoroaster or Charlemagne XI. on the bench, may be plain Jack or Ponto *en famille*. So with celebrities of the *genus homo*. Huxley's official style and appellation was "The Right Hon. Thomas Henry Huxley, P. C., M. D., Ph. D., LL. D., D. C. L., D. Sc., F. R. S.," and his biographer tells us that he delighted in its rolling grandeur—but to his wife he was always Hal. Shakespeare, to his fellows of his Bankside, was Will, and perhaps Willie to Ann Hathaway. The Kaiser is another Willie: the late Czar so addressed him in their famous exchange of telegrams. The Czar himself was Nicky in those days, and no doubt remains Nicky to his intimates today. Edgar Allan Poe was always Eddie to his wife, and Mark Twain was always Youth to his. P. T. Barnum's stable-name was Taylor, his middle name; Charles Lamb's was Guy; Nietzsche's was Fritz; Whistler's was Jimmie; the late King Edward's was Bertie; Grover Cleveland's was Steve; J. Pierpont Morgan's was Jack; Dr. Wilson's is Tom.

Some given names are surrounded by a whole flotilla of stable-names. Henry, for example, is softened variously into Harry, Hen, Hank, Hal, Henny, Enery, On'ry and Heinie. Which did Ann Boleyn use when she cooed into the suspicious ear of Henry VIII.? To which did Henrik Ibsen answer at the domestic hearth? It is difficult to imagine his wife calling him Henrik: the name is harsh, clumsy, razor-edged. But did she make it Hen or Rik, or neither? What was Bismarck to the Fürstin, and to the mother he so vastly feared? Ottchen? Somehow it seems impossible. What was Grant to his wife? Surely not Ulysses! And Wolfgang Amadeus Mozart? And Rutherford B. Hayes? Was Robert Browning ever Bob? Was John Wesley ever Jack? Was Emmanuel Swendenborg ever Manny? Was Tadeusz Kosciusko ever Teddy?

A fair field of inquiry invites. Let some laborious assistant professor explore and chart it. There will be more of human nature in his report than in all the novels ever written.

VIII
THE JEWS

The Jews, like the Americans, labor under a philosophical dualism, and in both cases it is a theological heritage. On the one hand there is the idealism that is lovely and uplifting and will get a man into heaven, and on the other hand there is the realism that works. The fact that the Jews cling to both, thus running, as it were, upon two tracks, is what makes them so puzzling, now and then, to the *goyim*. In one aspect they stand for the most savage practicality; in another aspect they are dreamers of an almost fabulous other-worldliness. My own belief is that the essential Jew is the idealist—that his occasional flashing of hyena teeth is no more than a necessary concession to the harsh demands of the struggle for existence. Perhaps, in many cases, it is due to an actual corruption of blood. The Jews come from the Levant, and their women were exposed for many centuries to the admiration of Greek, Arab and Armenian. The shark that a Jew can be at his worst is simply a Greek or Armenian at his best.

As a statement of post-mortem and super-terrestrial fact, the religion that the Jews have foisted upon the world seems to me to be as vast a curse as the influenza that we inherit from the Tatars or the democratic fallacies set afloat by the French Revolution. The one thing that can be said in favor of it is that it is not true, and yet we suffer from it almost as much as if it were true. But with it, encasing it and preserving it, there has come something that is positively valuable—something, indeed, that is beyond all price—and that is Jewish poetry. To compare it to the poetry of any other race is wholly impossible; it stands completely above all the rest; it is as far beyond the next best as German music is beyond French music, or French painting beyond English painting, or the English drama beyond the Italian drama. There are single chapters in the Old Testament that are worth all the poetry ever written in the New World and nine-tenths of that written in the Old. The Jews of those ancient days had imagination, they had dignity, they had ears for sweet sound, they had, above all, the faculty of grandeur. The stupendous music that issued from them has swept their barbaric demonology along with it, setting at naught the collective intelligence of the human species; they embalmed their idiotic taboos and fetishes in undying strains, and so gave them some measure of the same immortality. A race of lawgivers? Bosh! Leviticus is as archaic as the Code of Manu, and the Decalogue is a fossil. A race of seers? Bosh again! The God they saw survives only as a bogey-man, a theory, an uneasy and vexatious ghost. A race of traders and sharpers? Bosh a third time! The Jews are as poor as the Spaniards. But a race of poets, my lords, a race of poets! It is a vision of beauty that has ever haunted them. And it has been their destiny to transmit that vision, enfeebled, perhaps, but still distinct, to other and lesser peoples, that life might be made softer for the sons of men, and the goodness of the Lord God—whoever He may be—might not be forgotten.

IX
THE COMSTOCKIAN PREMISS

It is argued against certain books, by virtuosi of moral alarm, that they depict vice as attractive. This recalls the king who hanged a judge for deciding that an archbishop was a mammal.

X
THE LABIAL INFAMY

After five years of search I have been able to discover but one book in English upon the art of kissing, and that is a very feeble treatise by a savant of York, Pa., Dr. R. McCormick Sturgeon. There may be others, but I have been quite unable to find them. Kissing, for all one hears of it, has not attracted the scientists and literati; one compares its meagre literature with the endless books upon the other phenomena of love, especially divorce and obstetrics. Even Dr. Sturgeon, pioneering bravely, is unable to get beyond a sentimental and trivial view of the thing he vivisects, and so his book is no more than a compendium of mush. His very description of the act of kissing is made up of sonorous gabble about heaving bosoms, red lips, electric sparks and such-like imaginings. What reason have we for believing, as he says, that the lungs are "strongly expanded" during the act? My own casual observation inclines me to hold that the opposite is true, that the lungs are actually collapsed in a pseudo-asthmatic spasm. Again, what is the ground for arguing that the lips are "full, ripe and red?" The real effect of the emotions that accompany kissing is to empty the superficial capillaries and so produce a leaden pallor. As for such salient symptoms as the temperature, the pulse and the rate of respiration, the learned pundit passes them over without a word. Mrs. Elsie Clews Parsons would be a good one to write a sober and accurate treatise upon kissing. Her books upon "The Family" and "Fear and Conventionality" indicate her possession of the right sort of learning. Even better would be a work by Havelock Ellis, say, in three or four volumes. Ellis has devoted his whole life to illuminating the mysteries of sex, and his collection of materials is unsurpassed in the world. Surely there must be an enormous mass of instructive stuff about kissing in his card indexes, letter files, book presses and archives.

Just why the kiss as we know it should have attained to its present popularity in Christendom is probably one of the things past finding out. The Japanese, a very affectionate and sentimental people, do not practise kissing in any form; they regard the act, in fact, with an aversion matching our own aversion to the rubbing of noses. Nor is it in vogue among the Moslems, nor among the Chinese, who countenance it only as between mother and child. Even in parts of Christendom it is girt about by rigid taboos, so that its practise tends to be restricted to a few occasions. Two Frenchmen or Italians, when they meet, kiss each other on both cheeks. One used to see, indeed, many pictures of General Joffre thus bussing the heroes of Verdun; there even appeared in print a story to the effect that one of them objected to the scratching of his moustache. But imagine two Englishmen kissing! Or two Germans! As well imagined the former kissing the latter! Such a display of affection is simply impossible to men of Northern blood; they would die with shame if caught at it. The Englishman, like the American, never kisses if he can help it. He even regards it as bad form to kiss his wife in a railway station, or, in fact, anywhere in sight of a third party. The Latin has no such compunctions. He leaps to the business regardless of place or time; his sole concern is with the lady. Once, in driving from Nice to Monte Carlo along the lower Corniche road, I passed a hundred or so open taxicabs containing man and woman, and fully 75 per cent. of the men had their arms around their companions, and were kissing them. These were not peasants, remember, but well-to-do persons. In England such a scene would have caused a great scandal; in most American States the police would have charged the offenders with drawn revolvers.

The charm of kissing is one of the things I have always wondered at. I do not pretend, of course, that I have never done it; mere politeness forces one to it; there are women who sulk and grow bellicose unless one at least makes the motions of kissing them. But what I mean is that I have never found the act a tenth part as agreeable as poets, the authors of musical comedy librettos, and (on the contrary side) chaperones and the *gendarmerie* make it out. The physical sensation, far from being pleasant, is intensely uncomfortable—the suspension of respiration, indeed, quickly resolves itself into a feeling of suffocation—and the posture necessitated by the approximation of lips and lips is unfailingly a constrained and ungraceful one. Theoretically, a man kisses a woman perpendicularly, with their eyes, those "windows of the soul," synchronizing exactly. But actually, on account of the incompressibility of the nasal cartilages, he has to incline either his or her head to an angle of at least 60 degrees, and the result is that his right eye gazes insanely at the space between her eyebrows, while his left eye is fixed upon some vague spot behind her. An instantaneous photograph of such a maneuvre, taken at the moment of incidence, would probably turn the stomach of even the most romantic man, and force him, in sheer self-respect, to renounce kissing as he has renounced leap-frog and walking on stilts. Only a woman (for women are quite devoid of aesthetic feeling) could survive so damning a picture.

But the most embarrassing moment, in kissing, does not come during the actual kiss (for at that time the sensation of suffocation drives out all purely psychical feelings), but immediately afterward. What is one to say to the woman then? The occasion obviously demands some sort of remark. One has just received (in theory) a great boon; the silence begins to make itself felt; there stands the fair one, obviously waiting. Is one to thank her? Certainly that would be too transparent a piece of hypocrisy, too flaccid a banality. Is one to tell her that one loves her? Obviously, there is danger in such assurances, and beside, one usually doesn't, and a lie is a lie. Or is one to descend to chatty commonplaces—about the weather, literature, politics, the war? The practical impossibility of solving the problem leads almost inevitably to a blunder far worse than any merely verbal one: one kisses her again, and then again, and so on, and so on. The ultimate result is satiety, repugnance, disgust; even the girl herself gets enough.

XI
A TRUE ASCETIC

Herbert Spencer's objection to swearing, of which so much has been made by moralists, was not an objection to its sinfulness but an objection to its charm. In brief, he feared comfort, satisfaction, joy. The boarding houses in which he dragged out his gray years were as bare and cheerless as so many piano boxes. He avoided all the little vices and dissipations which make human existence bearable: good eating, good drinking, dancing, tobacco, poker, poetry, the theatre, personal adornment, philandering, adultery. He was insanely suspicious of everything that threatened to interfere with his work. Even when that work halted him by the sheer agony of its monotony, and it became necessary for him to find recreation, he sought out some recreation that was as unattractive as possible, in the hope that it would quickly drive him back to work again. Having to choose between methods of locomotion on his holidays, he chose going afoot, the most laborious and least satisfying available. Brought to bay by his human need for a woman, he directed his fancy toward George Eliot, probably the most unappetizing woman of his race and time. Drawn irresistibly to music, he avoided the Fifth Symphony and "Tristan und Isolde," and joined a crowd of old maids singing part songs around a cottage piano. John Tyndall saw clearly the effect of all this and protested against it, saying, "He'd be a much nicer fellow if he had a good swear now and then"—*i. e.*, if he let go now and then, if he yielded to his healthy human instincts now and then, if he went on some sort of debauch now and then. But what Tyndall overlooked was the fact that the meagreness of his recreations was the very element that attracted Spencer to them. Obsessed by the fear—and it turned out to be well-grounded—that he would not live long enough to complete his work, he regarded all joy as a temptation, a corruption, a sin of scarlet. He was a true ascetic. He could sacrifice all things of the present for one thing of the future, all things real for one thing ideal.

XII
ON LYING

Lying stands on a different plane from all other moral offenses, not because it is intrinsically more heinous or less heinous, but simply because it is the only one that may be accurately measured. Forgetting unwitting error, which has nothing to do with morals, a statement is either true or not true. This is a simple distinction and relatively easy to establish. But when one comes to other derelictions the thing grows more complicated. The line between stealing and not stealing is beautifully vague; whether or not one has crossed it is not determined by the objective act, but by such delicate things as motive and purpose. So again, with assault, sex offenses, and even murder; there may be surrounding circumstances which greatly condition the moral quality of the actual act. But lying is specific, exact, scientific. Its capacity for precise determination, indeed, makes its presence or non-presence the only accurate gauge of other immoral acts. Murder, for example, is nowhere regarded as immoral save it involve some repudiation of a social compact, of a tacit promise to refrain from it—in brief, some deceit, some perfidy, some lie. One may kill freely when the pact is formally broken, as in war. One may kill equally freely when it is broken by the victim, as in an assault by a highwayman. But one may not kill so long as it is not broken, and one may not break it to clear the way. Some form of lie is at the bottom of all other recognized crimes, from seduction to embezzlement. Curiously enough, this master immorality of them all is not prohibited by the Ten Commandments, nor is it penalized, in its pure form, by the code of any civilized nation. Only savages have laws against lying *per se.*

XIII
HISTORY

It is the misfortune of humanity that its history is chiefly written by third-rate men. The first-rate man seldom has any impulse to record and philosophise; his impulse is to act; life, to him, is an adventure, not a syllogism or an autopsy. Thus the writing of history is left to college professors, moralists, theorists, dunder-heads. Few historians, great or small, have shown any capacity for the affairs they presume to describe and interpret. Gibbon was an inglorious failure as a member of Parliament. Thycydides made such a mess of his military (or, rather, naval) command that he was exiled from Athens for twenty years and finally assassinated. Flavius Josephus, serving as governor of Galilee, lost the whole province to the Romans, and had to flee for his life. Momssen, elected to the Prussian Landtag, flirted with the Socialists. How much better we would understand the habits and nature of man if there were more historians like Julius Caesar, or even like Niccolo Machiavelli! Remembering the sharp and devastating character of their rough notes, think what marvelous histories Bismarck, Washington and Frederick the Great might have written! Such men are privy to the facts; the usual historians have to depend on deductions, rumors, guesses. Again, such men know how to tell the truth, however unpleasant; they are wholly free of that puerile moral obsession which marks the professor . . . But they so seldom tell it! Well, perhaps some of them have—and their penalty is that they are damned and forgotten.

XIV
THE CURSE OF CIVILIZATION

A civilized man's worst curse is social obligation. The most unpleasant act imaginable is to go to a dinner party. One could get far better food, taking one day with another, at Childs', or even in a Pennsylvania Railroad dining-car; one could find far more amusing society in a bar-room or a bordello, or even at the Y. M. C. A. No hostess in Christendom ever arranged a dinner party of any pretensions without including at least one intensely disagreeable person—a vain and vapid girl, a hideous woman, a follower of baseball, a stock-broker, a veteran of some war or other, a gabbler of politics. And one is enough to do the business.

XV
EUGENICS

The error of the eugenists lies in the assumption that a physically healthy man is the best fitted to survive. This is true of rats and the *pediculae*, but not of the higher animals, *e. g.*, horses, dogs and men. In these higher animals one looks for more subtle qualities, chiefly of the spirit. Imagine estimating philosophers by their chest expansions, their blood pressures, their Wassermann reactions!

The so-called social diseases, over which eugenists raise such a pother, are surely not the worst curses that mankind has to bear. Some of the greatest men in history have had them; whole nations have had them and survived. The truth about them is that, save in relatively rare cases, they do very little damage. The horror in which they are held is chiefly a moral horror, and its roots lie in the assumption that they cannot be contracted without sin. Nothing could be more false. Many great moralists have suffered from them: the gods are always up to such sardonic waggeries.

Moreover, only one of them is actually inheritable, and that one is transmitted relatively seldom. But among psychic characters one finds that practically all are inheritable. For example, stupidity, credulity, avarice, pecksniffery, lack of imagination, hatred of beauty, meanness, poltroonry, petty brutality, smallness of soul . . . I here present, of course, the Puritan complex; there flashes up the image of the "good man," that libel on God and the devil. Consider him well. If you had to choose a sire for a first-rate son, would you choose a consumptive Jew with the fires of eternity in his eyes, or an Iowa right-thinker with his hold full of Bibles and breakfast food?

XVI
THE JOCOSE GODS

What humor could be wilder than that of life itself? Franz Schubert, on his deathbed, read the complete works of J. Fenimore Cooper. John Millington Synge wrote "Riders to the Sea" on a second-hand $40 typewriter, and wore a celluloid collar. Richard Wagner made a living, during four lean years, arranging Italian opera arias for the cornet. Herbert Spencer sang bass in a barber-shop quartette and was in love with George Eliot. William Shakespeare was a social pusher and bought him a bogus coat-of-arms. Martin Luther suffered from the jim-jams. One of the greatest soldiers in Hungarian history was named Hunjadi Janos . . .

XVII
WAR

Superficially, war seems inordinately cruel and wasteful, and yet it must be plain on reflection that the natural evolutionary process is quite as cruel and even more wasteful. Man's chief efforts in times of peace are devoted to making that process less violent and sanguinary. Civilization, indeed, may be defined as a constructive criticism of nature, and Huxley even called it a conspiracy against nature. Man tries to remedy what must inevitably seem the mistakes and to check what must inevitably seem the wanton cruelty of the Creator. In war man abandons these efforts, and so becomes more jovian. The Greeks never represented the inhabitants of Olympus as succoring and protecting one another, but always as fighting and attempting to destroy one another.

No form of death inflicted by war is one-half so cruel as certain forms of death that are seen in hospitals every day. Besides, these forms of death have the further disadvantage of being inglorious. The average man, dying in bed, not only has to stand the pains and terrors of death; he must also, if he can bring himself to think of it at all, stand the notion that he is ridiculous . . . The soldier is at least not laughed at. Even his enemies treat his agonies with respect.

XVIII
MORALIST AND ARTIST

I dredge up the following from an essay on George Bernard Shaw by Robert Blatchford, the English Socialist: "Shaw is something much better than a wit, much better than an artist, much better than a politician or a dramatist; he is a moralist, a teacher of ethics, austere, relentless, fiercely earnest."

What could be more idiotic? Then Cotton Mather was a greater man than Johann Sebastian Bach. Then the average college critic of the arts, with his balderdash about inspiration and moral purpose, is greater than Georg Brandes or Saint-Beuve. Then Éugene Brieux, with his Y. M. C. A. platitudinizing, is greater than Molière, with his ethical agnosticism, his ironical determinism.

This childish respect for moralizing runs through the whole of contemporary criticism—at least in England and America. Blatchford differs from the professorial critics only in the detail that he can actually write. What he says about Shaw has been said, in heavy and suffocating words, by almost all of them. And yet nothing could be more untrue.

The moralist, at his best, can never be anything save a sort of journalist. Moral values change too often to have any serious validity or interest; what is a virtue today is a sin tomorrow. But the man who creates a thing of beauty creates something that lasts.

XIX
ACTORS

"In France they call an actor a *m'as-tu-vu*, which, anglicised, means a have-you-seen-me? . . . The average actor holds the mirror up to nature and sees in it only the reflection of himself." I take the words from a late book on the so-called art of the mime by the editor of a magazine devoted to the stage. The learned author evades plumbing the psychological springs of this astounding and almost invariable vanity, this endless bumptiousness of the *cabotin* in all climes and all ages. His one attempt is banal: "a foolish public makes much of him." With all due respect, Nonsense! The larval actor is full of hot and rancid gases long before a foolish public has had a fair chance to make anything of him at all, and he continues to emit them long after it has tried him, condemned him and bidden him be damned. There is, indeed, little choice in the virulence of their self-respect between a Broadway star who is slobbered over by press agents and fat women, and the poor ham who plays thinking parts in a No. 7 road company. The two are alike charged to the limit; one more ohm, or molecule, and they would burst. Actors begin where militia colonels, Fifth avenue rectors and Chautauqua orators leave off. The most modest of them (barring, perhaps, a few unearthly traitors to the craft) matches the conceit of the solitary pretty girl on a slow ship. In their lofty eminence of pomposity they are challenged only by Anglican bishops and grand opera tenors. I have spoken of the danger they run of bursting. In the case of tenors it must sometimes actually happen; even the least of them swells visibly as he sings, and permanently as he grows older . . .

But why are actors, in general, such blatant and obnoxious asses, such arrant posturers and wind-bags? Why is it as surprising to find an unassuming and likable fellow among them as to find a Greek without fleas? The answer is quite simple. To reach it one needs but consider the type of young man who normally gets stage-struck. Is he, taking averages, the intelligent, alert, ingenious, ambitious young fellow? Is he the young fellow with ideas in him, and a yearning for hard and difficult work? Is he the diligent reader, the hard student, the eager inquirer? No. He is, in the overwhelming main, the neighborhood fop and beau, the human clothes-horse, the nimble squire of dames. The youths of more active mind, emerging from adolescence, turn to business and the professions; the men that they admire and seek to follow are men of genuine distinction, men who have actually done difficult and valuable things, men who have fought good (if often dishonest) fights and are respected and envied by other men. The stage-struck youth is of a softer and more shallow sort. He seeks, not a chance to test his mettle by hard and useful work, but an easy chance to shine. He craves the regard, not of men, but of women. He is, in brief, a hollow and incompetent creature, a strutter and poseur, a popinjay, a pretty one . . .

I thus beg the question, but explain the actor. He is this silly youngster grown older, but otherwise unchanged. An initiate of a profession requiring little more information, culture or capacity for ratiocination than that of the lady of joy, and surrounded in his work-shop by men who are as stupid, as vain and as empty as he himself will be in the years to come, he suffers an arrest of development, and the little intelligence that may happen to be in him gets no chance to show itself. The result, in its usual manifestation, is the average bad actor—a man with the cerebrum of a floor-walker and the vanity of a fashionable clergyman. The result, in its highest and holiest form is the actor-manager, with his retinue of press-agents, parasites and worshipping wenches—perhaps the most preposterous and awe-inspiring donkey that civilization has yet produced. To look for sense in a fellow of such equipment and such a history would be like looking for serviettes in a sailors' boarding-house.

By the same token, the relatively greater intelligence of actresses is explained. They are, at their worst, quite as bad as the generality of actors. There are she-stars who are all temperament and balderdash—intellectually speaking, beggars on horseback, servant girls well washed. But no one who knows anything about the stage need be told that it can show a great many more quick-minded and self-respecting women than intelligent men. And why? Simply because its women are recruited, in the main, from a class much above that which furnishes its men. It is, after all, not unnatural for a woman of considerable intelligence to aspire to the stage. It offers her, indeed, one of the most tempting careers that is open to her. She cannot hope to succeed in business, and in the other professions she is an unwelcome and much-scoffed-at intruder, but on the boards she can meet men on an equal footing. It is, therefore, no wonder that women of a relatively superior class often take to the business . . . Once they embrace it, their superiority to their male colleagues is quickly manifest. All movements against puerility and imbecility in the drama have originated, not with actors, but with actresses—that is, in so far as they have originated among stage folks at all. The Ibsen pioneers were such women as Helena Modjeska, Agnes Sorma and Janet Achurch; the men all hung back. Ibsen, it would appear, was aware of this superior alertness and took shrewd advantage of it. At all events, his most tempting acting parts are feminine ones.

The girls of the stage demonstrate this tendency against great difficulties. They have to carry a heavy handicap in the enormous number of women who seek the footlights merely to advertise their real profession, but despite all this, anyone who has the slightest acquaintance with stagefolk will testify that, taking one with another, the women have vastly more brains than the men and are appreciably less vain and idiotic. Relatively few actresses of any rank marry actors. They find close communion with the strutting brethren psychologically impossible.

Stock-brokers, dramatists and even theatrical managers are greatly to be preferred.

XX
THE CROWD

Gustave Le Bon and his school, in their discussions of the psychology of crowds, have put forward the doctrine that the individual man, cheek by jowl with the multitude, drops down an intellectual peg or two, and so tends to show the mental and emotional reactions of his inferiors. It is thus that they explain the well-known violence and imbecility of crowds. The crowd, as a crowd, performs acts that many of its members, as individuals, would never be guilty of. Its average intelligence is very low; it is inflammatory, vicious, idiotic, almost simian. Crowds, properly worked up by skilful demagogues, are ready to believe anything, and to do anything.

Le Bon, I daresay, is partly right, but also partly wrong. His theory is probably too flattering to the average numskull. He accounts for the extravagance of crowds on the assumption that the numskull, along with the superior man, is knocked out of his wits by suggestion—that he, too, does things in association that he would never think of doing singly. The fact may be accepted, but the reasoning raises a doubt. The numskull runs amuck in a crowd, not because he has been inoculated with new rascality by the mysterious crowd influence, but because his habitual rascality now has its only chance to function safely. In other words, the numskull is vicious, but a poltroon. He refrains from all attempts at lynching *a cappella*, not because it takes suggestion to make him desire to lynch, but because it takes the protection of a crowd to make him brave enough to try it.

What happens when a crowd cuts loose is not quite what Le Bon and his followers describe. The few superior men in it are not straightway reduced to the level of the underlying stoneheads. On the contrary, they usually keep their heads, and often make efforts to combat the crowd action. But the stoneheads are too many for them; the fence is torn down or the blackamoor is lynched. And why? Not because the stoneheads, normally virtuous, are suddenly criminally insane. Nay, but because they are suddenly conscious of the power lying in their numbers—because they suddenly realize that their natural viciousness and insanity may be safely permitted to function.

In other words, the particular swinishness of a crowd is permanently resident in the majority of its members—in all those members, that is, who are naturally ignorant and vicious—perhaps 95 per cent. All studies of mob psychology are defective in that they underestimate this viciousness. They are poisoned by the prevailing delusion that the lower orders of men are angels. This is nonsense. The lower orders of men are incurable rascals, either individually or collectively. Decency, self-restraint, the sense of justice, courage—these virtues belong only to a small minority of men. This minority never runs amuck. Its most distinguishing character, in truth, is its resistance to all running amuck. The third-rate man, though he may wear the false whiskers of a first-rate man, may always be detected by his inability to keep his head in the face of an appeal to his emotions. A whoop strips off his disguise.

XXI
AN AMERICAN PHILOSOPHER

As for William Jennings Bryan, of whom so much piffle, pro and con, has been written, the whole of his political philosophy may be reduced to two propositions, neither of which is true. The first is the proposition that the common people are wise and honest, and the second is the proposition that all persons who refuse to believe it are scoundrels. Take away the two, and all that would remain of Jennings would be a somewhat greasy bald-headed man with his mouth open.

XXII
CLUBS

Men's clubs have but one intelligible purpose: to afford asylum to fellows who haven't any girls. Hence their general gloom, their air of lost causes, their prevailing acrimony. No man would ever enter a club if he had an agreeable woman to talk to. This is particularly true of married men. Those of them that one finds in clubs answer to a general description: they have wives too unattractive to entertain them, and yet too watchful to allow them to seek entertainment elsewhere. The bachelors, in the main, belong to two classes: (a) those who have been unfortunate in amour, and are still too sore to show any new enterprise, and (b) those so lacking in charm that no woman will pay any attention to them. Is it any wonder that the men one thus encounters in clubs are stupid and miserable creatures, and that they find their pleasure in such banal sports as playing cards, drinking highballs, shooting pool, and reading the barber-shop weeklies? . . . The day a man's mistress is married one always finds him at his club.

XXIII
FIDELIS AD URNUM

Despite the common belief of women to the contrary, fully 95 per cent. of all married men, at least in America, are faithful to their wives. This, however, is not due to virtue, but chiefly to lack of courage. It takes more initiative and daring to start up an extra-legal affair than most men are capable of. They look and they make plans, but that is as far as they get. Another salient cause of connubial rectitude is lack of means. A mistress costs a great deal more than a wife; in the open market of the world she can get more. It is only the rare man who can conceal enough of his income from his wife to pay for a morganatic affair. And most of the men clever enough to do this are too clever to be intrigued.

I have said that 95 per cent. of married men are faithful. I believe the real proportion is nearer 99 per cent. What women mistake for infidelity is usually no more than vanity. Every man likes to be regarded as a devil of a fellow, and particularly by his wife. On the one hand, it diverts her attention from his more genuine shortcomings, and on the other hand it increases her respect for him. Moreover, it gives her a chance to win the sympathy of other women, and so satisfies that craving for martyrdom which is perhaps woman's strongest characteristic. A woman who never has any chance to suspect her husband feels cheated and humiliated. She is in the position of those patriots who are induced to enlist for a war by pictures of cavalry charges, and then find themselves told off to wash the general's underwear.

XXIV
A THEOLOGICAL MYSTERY

The moral order of the world runs aground on hay fever. Of what use is it? Why was it invented? Cancer and hydrophobia, at least, may be defended on the ground that they kill. Killing may have some benign purpose, some esoteric significance, some cosmic use. But hay fever never kills; it merely tortures. No man ever died of it. Is the torture, then, an end in itself? Does it break the pride of strutting, snorting man, and turn his heart to the things of the spirit? Nonsense! A man with hay fever is a natural criminal. He curses the gods, and defies them to kill him. He even curses the devil. Is its use, then, to prepare him for happiness to come—for the vast ease and comfort of convalescence? Nonsense again! The one thing he is sure of, the one thing he never forgets for a moment, is that it will come back again next year.

XXV
THE TEST OF TRUTH

The final test of truth is ridicule. Very few religious dogmas have ever faced it and survived. Huxley laughed the devils out of the Gadarene swine. Dowie's whiskers broke the back of Dowieism. Not the laws of the United States but the mother-in-law joke brought the Mormons to compromise and surrender. Not the horror of it but the absurdity of it killed the doctrine of infant damnation . . . But the razor edge of ridicule is turned by the tough hide of truth. How loudly the barber-surgeons laughed at Harvey—and how vainly! What clown ever brought down the house like Galileo? Or Columbus? Or Jenner? Or Lincoln? Or Darwin? . . . They are laughing at Nietzsche yet . . .

XXVI
LITERARY INDECENCIES

The low, graceless humor of names! On my shelf of poetry, arranged by the alphabet, Coleridge and J. Gordon Cooglar are next-door neighbors! Mrs. Hemans is beside Laurence Hope! Walt Whitman rubs elbows with Ella Wheeler Wilcox; Robert Browning with Richard Burton; Rossetti with Cale Young Rice; Shelly with Clinton Scollard; Wordsworth with George E. Woodberry; John Keats with Herbert Kaufman!

Ibsen, on the shelf of dramatists, is between Victor Hugo and Jerome K. Jerome. Sudermann follows Harriet Beecher Stowe. Maeterlinck shoulders Percy Mackaye. Shakespeare is between Sardou and Shaw. Euripides and Clyde Fitch! Upton Sinclair and Sophocles! Aeschylus and F. Anstey! D'Annunzio and Richard Harding Davis! Augustus Thomas and Tolstoi!

More alphabetical humor. Gerhart Hauptmann and Robert Hichens; Voltaire and Henry Van Dyke; Flaubert and John Fox, Jr.; Balzac and John Kendrick Bangs; Ostrovsky and E. Phillips Oppenheim; Elinor

Glyn and Théophile Gautier; Joseph Conrad and Robert W. Chambers; Zola and Zangwill! . . .

Midway on my scant shelf of novels, between George Moore and Frank Norris, there is just room enough for the two volumes of "Derringforth," by Frank A. Munsey.

XXVII
VIRTUOUS VANDALISM

A hearing of Schumann's B flat symphony of late, otherwise a very caressing experience, was corrupted by the thought that music would be much the gainer if musicians could get over their superstitious reverence for the mere text of the musical classics. That reverence, indeed, is already subject to certain limitations; hands have been laid, at one time or another, upon most of the immortal oratorios, and even the awful name of Bach has not dissuaded certain German editors. But it still swathes the standard symphonies like some vast armor of rubber and angel food, and so imagination has to come to the aid of the flutes and fiddles when the band plays Schumann, Mozart, and even parts of Beethoven. One discerns, often quite clearly, what the reverend Master was aiming at, but just as often one fails to hear it in precise tones.

This is particularly true of Schumann, whose deficiency in instrumental cunning has passed into proverb. And in the B flat symphony, his first venture into the epic form, his failures are most numerous. More than once, obviously attempting to roll up tone into a moving climax, he succeeds only in muddling his colors. I remember one place—at the moment I can't recall where it is—where the strings and the brass storm at one another in furious figures. The blast of the brass, as the vaudevillains say, gets across—but the fiddles merely scream absurdly. The whole passage suggests the bleating of sheep in the midst of a vast bellowing of bulls. Schumann overestimated the horsepower of fiddle music so far up the E string—or underestimated the full kick of the trumpets . . . Other such soft spots are well known.

Why, then, go on parroting *gaucheries* that Schumann himself, were he alive today, would have long since corrected? Why not call an ecumenical council, appoint a commission to see to such things, and then forget the sacrilege? As a self-elected delegate from heathendom, I nominate Dr. Richard Strauss as chairman. When all is said and done, Strauss probably knows more about writing for orchestra than any other two men that ever lived, not excluding Wagner. Surely no living rival, as Dr. Sunday would say, has anything on him. If, after hearing a new composition by Strauss, one turns to the music, one is invariably surprised to find how simple it is. The performance reveals so many purple moments, so staggering an array of lusciousness, that the ear is bemused into detecting scales and chords that never were on land or sea. What the exploratory eye subsequently discovers, perhaps, is no more than our stout and comfortable old friend, the highly well-born *hausfrau*, Mme. C Dur—with a vine leaf or two of C sharp minor or F major in her hair. The trick lies in the tone-color—in the flabbergasting magic of the orchestration. There are some moments in "Elektra" when sounds come out of the orchestra that tug at the very roots of the hair, sounds so unearthly that they suggest a caroling of dragons or *bierfisch*—and yet they are made by the same old fiddles that play the Kaiser Quartet, and by the same old trombones that the Valkyrie ride like witch's broomsticks, and by the same old flutes that sob and snuffle in Tit'l's Serenade. And in parts of "Feuersnot"—but Roget must be rewritten by Strauss before "Feuersnot" is described. There is one place where the harps, taking a running start from the scrolls of the violins, leap slambang through (or is it into?) the firmament of Heaven. Once, when I heard this passage played at a concert, a woman sitting beside me rolled over like a log, and had to be hauled out by the ushers.

Yes; Strauss is the man to reorchestrate the symphonies of Schumann, particularly the B flat, the Rhenish and the Fourth. I doubt that he could do much with Schubert, for Schubert, though he is dead nearly a hundred years, yet remains curiously modern. The Unfinished symphony is full of exquisite color effects—consider, for example, the rustling figure for the strings in the first movement—and as for the C major, it is so stupendous a debauch of melodic and harmonic beauty that one scarcely notices the colors at all. In its slow movement mere loveliness in music probably says all that will ever be said . . . But what of old Ludwig? Har, har; here we begin pulling the whiskers of Baal Himself. Nevertheless, I am vandal enough to wonder, on sad Sunday mornings, what Strauss could do with the first movement of the C minor. More, if Strauss ever does it and lets me hear the result just once, I'll be glad to serve six months in jail with him . . . But in Munich, of course! And with a daily visitor's pass for Cousin Pschorr! . . .

The conservatism which shrinks at such barbarities is the same conservatism which demands that the very typographical errors in the Bible be swallowed without salt, and that has thus made a puerile dream-book of parts of Holy Writ. If you want to see how far this last madness has led Christendom astray, take a look at an article by Abraham Mitrie Rihbany, an intelligent Syrian, in the *Atlantic Monthly* of a couple of years ago. The title of the article is "The Oriental Manner of Speech," and in it Rihbany shows how much of mere Oriental extravagance of metaphor is to be found in many celebrated passages, and how little of literal significance. This Oriental extravagance, of course, makes for beauty, but as interpreted by pundits of no imagination it surely doesn't make for understanding. What the Western World needs is a Bible in which the idioms of the Aramaic of thousands of years ago are translated into the idioms of today. The man who undertook such a translation, to be sure, would be uproariously denounced, just as Luther and Wycliffe were denounced, but he could well afford to face the storm. The various Revised Versions, including the Modern Speech New Testament of Richard Francis Weymouth, leave much to be desired. They rectify many naif blunders and so make the whole narrative more intelligible, but they still render most of the tropes of the original literally.

These tropes are not the substance of Holy Writ; they are simply its color. In the same way mere tone-color is not the substance of a musical composition. Beethoven's Eighth Symphony is just as great a work, in all its essentials, in a four-hand piano arrangement as in the original score. Every harmonic and melodic idea of the composer is there; one can trace just as clearly the subtle processes of his mind; every step in the working out of the materials is just as plain. True enough, there are orchestral compositions of which this cannot be reasonably said; their color is so much more important than their form that when one takes away the former the latter almost ceases to exist. But I doubt that many competent critics would argue that they belong to the first rank. Form, after all, is the important thing. It is design that counts, not decoration—design and organization. The pillars of a musical masterpiece are like the pillars of the Parthenon; they are almost as beautiful bleached white as they were in all their original hues.

XXVIII
A FOOTNOTE ON THE DUEL OF SEX

If I were a woman I should want to be a blonde, with golden, silky hair, pink cheeks and sky-blue eyes. It would not bother me to think that this color scheme was mistaken by the world for a flaunting badge of stupidity; I would have a better arm in my arsenal than mere intelligence; I would get a husband by easy surrender while the brunettes attempted it vainly by frontal assault.

Men are not easily taken by frontal assault; it is only strategem that can quickly knock them down. To be a blonde, pink, soft and delicate, is to be a strategem. It is to be a ruse, a feint, an ambush. It is to fight under the Red Cross flag. A man sees nothing alert and designing in those pale, crystalline eyes; he sees only something helpless, childish, weak; something that calls to his compassion; something that appeals powerfully to his conceit in his own strength. And so he is taken before he knows that there is a war. He lifts his portcullis in Christian charity—and the enemy is in his citadel.

The brunette can make no such stealthy and sure attack. No matter how subtle her art, she can never hope to quite conceal her intent. Her eyes give her away. They flash and glitter. They have depths. They draw the male gaze into mysterious and sinister recesses. And so the male behind the gaze flies to arms. He may be taken in the end—indeed, he usually is—but he is not taken by surprise; he is not taken without a fight. A brunette has to battle for every inch of her advance. She is confronted by an endless succession of Dead Man's Hills, each equipped with telescopes, semaphores, alarm gongs, wireless. The male sees her clearly through her densest smoke-clouds . . . But the blonde captures him under a flag of truce. He regards her tenderly, kindly, almost pityingly, until the moment the gyves are upon his wrists.

It is all an optical matter, a question of color. The pastel shades deceive him; the louder hues send him to his artillery. God help, I say, the red-haired girl! She goes into action with warning pennants flying. The dullest, blindest man can see her a mile away; he can catch the alarming flash of her hair long before he can see the whites, or even the terrible red-browns, of her eyes. She has a long field to cross, heavily under defensive fire, before she can get into rifle range. Her quarry has a chance to throw up redoubts, to dig himself in, to call for reinforcements, to elude her by ignominious flight. She must win, if she is to win at all, by an unparalleled combination of craft and resolution. She must be swift, daring, merciless. Even the brunette of black and penetrating eye has great advantages over her. No wonder she never lets go, once her arms are around her antagonist's neck! No wonder she is, of all women, the hardest to shake off!

All nature works in circles. Causes become effects; effects develop into causes. The red-haired girl's dire need of courage and cunning has augmented her store of those qualities by the law of natural selection. She is, by long odds, the most intelligent and bemusing of women. She shows cunning, foresight, technique, variety. She always fails a dozen times before she succeeds; but she brings to the final business the abominable expertness of a Ludendorff; she has learnt painfully by the process of trial and error. Red-haired girls are intellectual stimulants. They know all the tricks. They are so clever that they have even cast a false glamour of beauty about their worst defect—their harsh and gaudy hair. They give it euphemistic and deceitful names—auburn, bronze, Titian. They overcome by their hellish arts that deep-seated dread of red which is inborn in all of God's creatures. They charm men with what would even alarm bulls.

And the blondes, by following the law of least resistance, have gone in the other direction. The great majority of them—I speak, of course, of natural blondes; not of the immoral wenches who work their atrocities under cover of a synthetic blondeness—are quite as shallow and stupid as they look. One seldom hears a blonde say anything worth hearing; the most they commonly achieve is a specious, baby-like prattling, an infantile artlessness. But let us not blame them for nature's work. Why, after all, be intelligent? It is, at best, no more than a capacity for unhappiness. The blonde not only doesn't miss it; she is even better off without it. What imaginable intelligence could compensate her for the flat blueness of her eyes, the xanthous pallor of her hair, the doll-like pink of her cheeks? What conceivable cunning could do such execution as her stupendous appeal to masculine vanity, sentimentality, egoism?

If I were a woman I should want to be a blonde. My blondeness might be hideous, but it would get me a husband, and it would make him cherish me and love me.

XXIX
ALCOHOL

Envy, as I have said, is at the heart of the messianic delusion, the mania to convert the happy sinner into a "good" man, and so make him miserable. And at the heart of that envy is fear—the fear to sin, to take a chance, to monkey with the buzzsaw. This ineradicable fear is the outstanding mark of the fifth-rate man, at all times and everywhere. It dominates his politics, his theology, his whole thinking. He is a moral fellow because he is afraid to venture over the fence—and he hates the man who is not.

The solemn proofs, so laboriously deduced from life insurance statistics, that the man who uses alcohol, even moderately, dies slightly sooner than the teetotaler—these proofs merely show that this man is one who leads an active and vigorous life, and so faces hazards and uses himself up—in brief, one who lives at high tempo and with full joy, what Nietzsche used to call the *ja-sager*, or yes-sayer. He may, in fact, die slightly sooner than the teetotaler, but he lives infinitely longer. Moreover, his life, humanly speaking, is much more worth while, to himself and to the race. He does the hard and dangerous work of the world, he takes the chances, he makes the experiments. He is the soldier, the artist, the innovator, the lover. All the great works of man have been done by men who thus lived joyously, strenuously, and perhaps a bit dangerously. They have never been concerned about stretching life for two or three more years; they have been concerned about making life engrossing and stimulating and a high adventure while it lasts. Teetotalism is as impossible to such men as any other manifestation of cowardice, and, if it were possible, it would destroy their utility and significance just as certainly.

A man who shrinks from a cocktail before dinner on the ground that it may flabbergast his hormones, and so make him die at 69 years, ten months and five days instead of at 69 years, eleven months and seven days—such a man is as absurd a poltroon as the fellow who shrinks from kissing a woman on the ground that she may floor him with a chair leg. Each flees from a purely theoretical risk. Each is a useless encumberer of the earth, and the sooner dead the better. Each is a discredit to the human race, already discreditable enough, God knows.

Teetotalism does not make for human happiness; it makes for the dull, idiotic happiness of the barnyard. The men who do things in the world, the men worthy of admiration and imitation, are men constitutionally incapable of any such pecksniffian stupidity. Their ideal is not a safe life, but a full life; they do not try to follow the canary bird in a cage, but the eagle in the air. And in particular they do not flee from shadows and bugaboos. The alcohol myth is such a bugaboo. The sort of man it scares is the sort of man whose chief mark is that he is always scared.

No wonder the Rockefellers and their like are hot for saving the workingman from John Barleycorn! Imagine the advantage to them of operating upon a flabby horde of timorous and joyless slaves, afraid of all fun and kicking up, horribly moral, eager only to live as long as possible! What mule-like fidelity and efficiency could be got out of such a rabble! But how many Lincolns would you get out of it, and how many Jacksons, and how many Grants?

XXX
THOUGHTS ON THE VOLUPTUOUS

Why has no publisher ever thought of perfuming his novels? The final refinement of publishing, already bedizened by every other art! Barabbas turned Petronius! For instance, consider the bucolic romances of the hyphenated Mrs. Porter. They have a subtle flavor of new-mown hay and daffodils already; why not add the actual essence, or at all events some safe coal-tar substitute, and so help imagination to spread its wings? For Hall Caine, musk and synthetic bergamot. For Mrs. Glyn and her neighbors on the tiger-skin, the fragrant blood of the red, red rose. For the ruffianish pages of Jack London, the pungent, hospitable smell of a first-class bar-room—that indescribable mingling of Maryland rye, cigar smoke, stale malt liquor, radishes, potato salad and *blutwurst*. For the Dartmoor sagas of the interminable Phillpotts, the warm ammoniacal bouquet of cows, poultry and yokels. For the "Dodo" school, violets and Russian cigarettes. For the venerable Howells, lavender and mignonette. For Zola, Rochefort and wet leather. For Mrs. Humphrey Ward, lilies of the valley. For Marie Corelli, tuberoses and embalming fluid. For Chambers, sachet and lip paint. For—

But I leave you to make your own choices. All I offer is the general idea. It has been tried in the theatre. Well do I remember the first weeks of "Florodora" at the old Casino, with a mannikin in the lobby squirting "La Flor de Florodora" upon all us Florodorans . . . I was put on trial for my life when I got home!

XXXI
THE HOLY ESTATE

Marriage is always a man's second choice. It is entered upon, more often than not, as the safest form of intrigue. The caitiff yields quickest; the man who loves danger and adventure holds out longest. Behind it one frequently finds, not that lofty romantic passion which poets hymn, but a mere yearning for peace and security. The abominable hazards of the high seas, the rough humors and pestilences of the forecastle—these drive the timid mariner ashore . . . The authentic Cupid, at least in Christendom, was discovered by the late Albert Ludwig Siegmund Neisser in 1879.

XXXII
DICHTUNG UND WAHRHEIT

Deponent, being duly sworn, saith: My taste in poetry is for delicate and fragile things—to be honest, for artificial things. I like a frail but perfectly articulated stanza, a sonnet wrought like ivory, a song full of glowing nouns, verbs, adjectives, adverbs, pronouns, conjunctions, prepositions and participles, but without too much hard sense to it. Poetry, to me, has but two meanings. On the one hand, it is a magical escape from the sordidness of metabolism and the class war, and on the other hand it is a subtle, very difficult and hence very charming art, like writing fugues or mixing mayonnaise. I do not go to poets to be taught anything, or to be heated up to indignation, or to have my conscience blasted out of its torpor, but to be soothed and caressed, to be lulled with sweet sounds, to be wooed into forgetfulness, to be tickled under the metaphysical chin. My favorite poem is Lizette Woodworth Reese's "Tears," which, as a statement of fact, seems to me to be as idiotic as the Book of Revelation. The poetry I regard least is such stuff as that of Robert Browning and Matthew Arnold, which argues and illuminates. I dislike poetry of intellectual content as much as I dislike women of intellectual content—and for the same reason.

XXXIII
WILD SHOTS

If I had the time, and there were no sweeter follies offering, I should like to write an essay on the books that have quite failed of achieving their original purposes, and are yet of respectable use and potency for other purposes. For example, the Book of Revelation. The obvious aim of the learned author of this work was to bring the early Christians into accord by telling them authoritatively what to expect and hope for; its actual effect during eighteen hundred years has been to split them into a multitude of camps, and so set them to denouncing, damning, jailing and murdering one another. Again, consider the autobiography of Benvenuto Cellini. Ben wrote it to prove that he was an honest man, a mirror of all the virtues, an injured innocent; the world, reading it, hails him respectfully as the noblest, the boldest, the gaudiest liar that ever lived. Again, turn to "Gulliver's Travels." The thing was planned by its rev. author as a devastating satire, a terrible piece of cynicism; it survives as a story-book for sucklings. Yet again, there is "Hamlet." Shakespeare wrote it frankly to make money for a theatrical manager; it has lost money for theatrical managers ever since. Yet again, there is Caesar's "De Bello Gallico." Julius composed it to thrill and arouse the Romans; its sole use today is to stupefy and sicken schoolboys. Finally, there is the celebrated book of General F. von Bernhardi. He wrote it to inflame Germany; its effect was to inflame England . . .

The list might be lengthened almost *ad infinitum*. When a man writes a book he fires a machine gun into a wood. The game he brings down often astonishes him, and sometimes horrifies him. Consider the case of Ibsen . . . After my book on Nietzsche I was actually invited to lecture at Princeton.

XXXIV
BEETHOVEN

Romain Rolland's "Beethoven," one of the cornerstones of his celebrity as a critic, is based upon a thesis that is of almost inconceivable inaccuracy, to wit, the thesis that old Ludwig was an apostle of joy, and that his music reveals his determination to experience and utter it in spite of all the slings and arrows of outrageous fortune. Nothing could be more absurd. Joy, in truth, was precisely the emotion that Beethoven could never conjure up; it simply was not in him. Turn to the *scherzo* of any of his trios, quartets, sonatas or symphonies. A sardonic waggishness is there, and sometimes even a wistful sort of merriment, but joy in the real sense—a kicking up of legs, a light-heartedness, a complete freedom from care—is not to be found. It is in Haydn, it is in Schubert and it is often in Mozart, but it is no more in Beethoven than it is in Tschaikovsky. Even the hymn to joy at the end of the Ninth symphony narrowly escapes being a gruesome parody on the thing itself; a conscious effort is in every note of it; it is almost as lacking in spontaneity as (if it were imaginable at all) a piece of *vers libre* by Augustus Montague Toplady.

Nay; Ludwig was no leaping buck. Nor was it his deafness, nor poverty, nor the crimes of his rascally nephew that pumped joy out of him. The truth is that he lacked it from birth; he was born a Puritan—and though a Puritan may also become a great man (as witness Herbert Spencer and Beelzebub), he can never throw off being a Puritan. Beethoven stemmed from the Low Countries, and the Low Countries, in those days, were full of Puritan refugees; the very name, in its first incarnation, may have been Barebones. If you want to comprehend the authentic man, don't linger over Rolland's fancies but go to his own philosophizings, as garnered in "Beethoven, the Man and the Artist," by Friedrich Kerst, Englished by Krehbiel. Here you will find a collection of moral banalities that would have delighted Jonathan Edwards—a collection that might well be emblazoned on gilt cards and hung in Sunday schools. He begins with a naif anthropomorphism that is now almost perished from the world; he ends with a solemn repudiation of adultery . . . But a great man, my masters, a great man! We have enough biographies of him, and talmuds upon his works. Who will do a full-length psychological study of him?

XXXV
THE TONE ART

The notion that the aim of art is to fix the shifting aspects of nature, that all art is primarily representative—this notion is as unsound as the theory that Friday is an unlucky day, and is dying as hard. One even finds some trace of it in Anatole France, surely a man who should know better. The true function of art is to criticise, embellish and edit nature—particularly to edit it, and so make it coherent and lovely. The artist is a sort of impassioned proof-reader, blue-pencilling the *lapsus calami* of God. The sounds in a Beethoven symphony, even the Pastoral, are infinitely more orderly, varied and beautiful than those of the woods. The worst flute is never as bad as the worst soprano. The best violoncello is immeasurably better than the best tenor.

All first-rate music suffers by the fact that it has to be performed by human beings—that is, that nature must be permitted to corrupt it. The performance one hears in a concert hall or opera house is no more than a baroque parody upon the thing the composer imagined. In an orchestra of eighty men there is inevitably at least one man with a sore thumb, or bad kidneys, or a brutal wife, or *katzenjammer*—and one is enough. Some day the natural clumsiness and imperfection of fingers, lips and larynxes will be overcome by mechanical devices, and we shall have Beethoven and Mozart and Schubert in such wonderful and perfect beauty that it will be almost unbearable. If half as much ingenuity had been lavished upon music machines as has been lavished upon the telephone and the steam engine, we would have had mechanical orchestras long ago. Mechanical pianos are already here. Piano-players, bound to put some value on the tortures of Czerny, affect to laugh at all such contrivances, but that is no more than a pale phosphorescence of an outraged *wille zur macht*. Setting aside half a dozen—perhaps a dozen—great masters of a moribund craft, who will say that the average mechanical piano is not as competent as the average pianist?

When the human performer of music goes the way of the galley-slave, the charm of personality, of course, will be pumped out of the performance of music. But the charm of personality does not help music; it hinders it. It is not a reinforcement to music; it is a rival. When a beautiful singer comes upon the stage, two shows, as it were, go on at once: first the music show, and then the arms, shoulders, neck, nose, ankles, eyes, hips, calves and ruby lips—in brief, the sex-show. The second of these shows, to the majority of persons present, is more interesting than the first—to the men because of the sex interest, and to the women because of the professional or technical interest—and so music is forced into the background. What it becomes, indeed, is no more than a half-heard accompaniment to an imagined anecdote, just as color, line and mass become mere accomplishments to an anecdote in a picture by an English academician, or by a sentimental German of the Boecklin school.

The purified and dephlogisticated music of the future, to be sure, will never appeal to the mob, which will keep on demanding its chance to gloat over gaudy, voluptuous women, and fat, scandalous tenors. The mob, even disregarding its insatiable appetite for the improper, is a natural hero worshiper. It loves, not the beautiful, but the strange, the unprecedented, the astounding; it suffers from an incurable *héliogabalisme*. A soprano who can gargle her way up to G sharp in altissimo interests it almost as much as a contralto who has slept publicly with a grand duke. If it cannot get the tenor who receives $3,000 a night, it will take the tenor who fought the manager with bung-starters last Tuesday. But this is merely saying that the tastes and desires of the mob have nothing to do with music as an art. For its ears, as for its eyes, it demands anecdotes—on the one hand the Suicide symphony, "The Forge in the Forest," and the general run of Italian opera, and on the other hand such things as "The Angelus," "Playing Grandpa" and the so-called "Mona Lisa." It cannot imagine art as devoid of moral content, as beauty pure and simple. It always demands something to edify it, or, failing that, to shock it.

These concepts, of the edifying and the shocking, are closer together in the psyche than most persons imagine. The one, in fact, depends upon the other: without some definite notion of the improving it is almost impossible to conjure up an active notion of the improper. All salacious art is addressed, not to the damned, but to the consciously saved; it is Sunday-school superintendents, not bartenders, who chiefly patronize peep-shows, and know the dirty books, and have a high artistic admiration for sopranos of superior gluteal development. The man who has risen above the petty ethical superstitions of Christendom gets little pleasure out of impropriety, for very few ordinary phenomena seem to him to be improper. Thus a Frenchman, viewing the undraped statues which bedizen his native galleries of art, either enjoys them in a purely aesthetic fashion—which is seldom possible save when he is in liquor—or confesses frankly that he doesn't like them at all; whereas the visiting Americano is so powerfully shocked and fascinated by them that one finds him, the same evening, in places where no respectable man ought to go. All art, to this fellow, must have a certain bawdiness, or he cannot abide it. His favorite soprano, in the opera house, is not the fat and middle-aged lady who can actually sing, but the girl with the bare back and translucent drawers. Condescending to the concert hall, he is bored by the posse of enemy aliens in funereal black, and so demands a vocal soloist—that is, a gaudy creature of such advanced corsetting that she can make him forget Bach for a while, and turn his thoughts pleasantly to amorous intrigue.

In all this, of course, there is nothing new. Other and better men have noted the damage that the personal equation does to music, and some of them have even sought ways out. For example, Richard Strauss. His so-called ballet, "Josefs Legend," produced in Paris just before the war, is an attempt to write an opera without singers. All of the music is in the orchestra; the folks on the stage merely go through a pointless pantomime; their main function is to entertain the eye with shifting colors. Thus, the romantic sentiments of Joseph are announced, not by some eye-rolling tenor, but by the first, second, third, fourth, fifth, sixth, seventh and eighth violins (it is a Strauss score!), with the incidental aid of the wood-wind, the brass, the percussion and the rest of the strings. And the heroine's reply is made, not by a soprano with a cold, but by an honest man playing a flute. The next step will be the substitution of marionettes for actors. The removal of the orchestra to a sort of trench, out of sight of the audience, is already an accomplished fact at Munich. The end, perhaps, will be music purged of its current ptomaines. In brief, music.

XXXVI
ZOOS

I often wonder how much sound and nourishing food is fed to the animals in the zoological gardens of America every week, and try to figure out what the public gets in return for the cost thereof. The annual bill must surely run into millions; one is constantly hearing how much beef a lion downs at a meal, and how many tons of hay an elephant dispatches in a month. And to what end? To the end, principally, that a horde of superintendents and keepers may be kept in easy jobs. To the end, secondarily, that the least intelligent minority of the population may have an idiotic show to gape at on Sunday afternoons, and that the young of the species may be instructed in the methods of amour prevailing among chimpanzees and become privy to the technic employed by jaguars, hyenas and polar bears in ridding themselves of lice.

So far as I can make out, after laborious visits to all the chief zoos of the nation, no other imaginable purpose is served by their existence. One hears constantly, true enough (mainly from the gentlemen they support) that they are educational. But how? Just what sort of instruction do they radiate, and what is its value? I have never been able to find out. The sober truth is that they are no more educational than so many firemen's parades or displays of sky-rockets, and that all they actually offer to the public in return for the taxes wasted upon them is a form of idle and witless amusement, compared to which a visit to a penitentiary, or even to Congress or a state legislature in session, is informing, stimulating and ennobling.

Education your grandmother! Show me a schoolboy who has ever learned anything valuable or important by watching a mangy old lion snoring away in its cage or a family of monkeys fighting for peanuts. To get any useful instruction out of such a spectacle is palpably impossible; not even a college professor is improved by it. The most it can imaginably impart is that the stripes of a certain sort of tiger run one way and the stripes of another sort some other way, that hyenas and polecats smell worse than Greek 'bus boys, that the Latin name of the raccoon (who was unheard of by the Romans) is *Procyon lotor*. For the dissemination of such banal knowledge, absurdly emitted and defectively taken in, the taxpayers of the United States are mulcted in hundreds of thousands of dollars a year. As well make them pay for teaching policemen the theory of least squares, or for instructing roosters in the laying of eggs.

But zoos, it is argued, are of scientific value. They enable learned men to study this or that. Again the facts blast the theory. No scientific discovery of any value whatsoever, even to the animals themselves, has ever come out of a zoo. The zoo scientist is the old woman of zoology, and his alleged wisdom is usually exhibited, not in the groves of actual learning, but in the yellow journals. He is to biology what the late Camille Flammarion was to astronomy, which is to say, its court jester and reductio ad absurdum. When he leaps into public notice with some new pearl of knowledge, it commonly turns out to be no more than the news that Marie Bashkirtseff, the Russian lady walrus, has had her teeth plugged with zinc and is expecting twins. Or that Pishposh, the man-eating alligator, is down with locomotor ataxia. Or that Damon, the grizzly, has just finished his brother Pythias in the tenth round, chewing off his tail, nose and remaining ear.

Science, of course, has its uses for the lower animals. A diligent study of their livers and lights helps to an understanding of the anatomy and physiology, and particularly of the pathology, of man. They are necessary aids in devising and manufacturing many remedial agents, and in testing the virtues of those already devised; out of the mute agonies of a rabbit or a calf may come relief for a baby with diphtheria, or means for an archdeacon to escape the consequences of his youthful follies. Moreover, something valuable is to be got out of a mere study of their habits, instincts and ways of mind—knowledge that, by analogy, may illuminate the parallel doings of the *genus homo*, and so enable us to comprehend the primitive mental processes of Congressmen, morons and the rev. clergy.

But it must be obvious that none of these studies can be made in a zoo. The zoo animals, to begin with, provide no material for the biologist; he can find out no more about their insides than what he discerns from a safe distance and through the bars. He is not allowed to try his germs and specifics upon them; he is not allowed to vivisect them. If he would find out what goes on in the animal body under this condition or that, he must turn from the inhabitants of the zoo to the customary guinea pigs and street dogs, and buy or steal them for himself. Nor does he get any chance for profitable inquiry when zoo animals die (usually of lack of exercise or ignorant doctoring), for their carcasses are not handed to him for autopsy, but at once stuffed with gypsum and excelsior and placed in some museum.

Least of all do zoos produce any new knowledge about animal behavior. Such knowledge must be got, not from animals penned up and tortured, but from animals in a state of nature. A college professor studying the habits of the giraffe, for example, and confining his observations to specimens in zoos, would inevitably come to the conclusion that the giraffe is a sedentary and melancholy beast, standing immovable for hours at a time and employing an Italian to feed him hay and cabbages. As well proceed to a study of the psychology of a juris-consult by first immersing him in Sing Sing, or of a juggler by first cutting off his hands. Knowledge so gained is inaccurate and imbecile knowledge. Not even a college professor, if sober, would give it any faith and credit.

There remains, then, the only true utility of a zoo: it is a childish and pointless show for the unintelligent, in brief, for children, nursemaids, visiting yokels and the generality of the defective. Should the taxpayers be forced to sweat millions for such a purpose? I think not. The sort of man who likes to spend his time watching a cage of monkeys chase one another, or a lion gnaw its tail, or a lizard catch flies, is precisely the sort of man whose mental weakness should be combatted at the public expense, and not fostered. He is a public liability and a public menace, and society should seek to improve him. Instead of that, we spend a lot of money to feed his degrading appetite and further paralyze his mind. It is precisely as if the community provided free champagne for dipsomaniacs, or hired lecturers to convert the army to the doctrines of the Bolsheviki.

Of the abominable cruelties practised in zoos it is unnecessary to make mention. Even assuming that all the keepers are men of delicate natures and ardent zoophiles (which is about as safe as assuming that the keepers of a prison are all sentimentalists, and weep for the sorrows of their charges), it must be plain that the work they do involves an endless war upon the native instincts of the animals, and that they must thus inflict the most abominable tortures every day. What could be a sadder sight than a tiger in a cage, save it be a forest monkey climbing dispairingly up a barked stump, or an eagle chained to its roost? How can man be benefitted and made better by robbing the seal of its arctic ice, the hippopotamus of its soft wallow, the buffalo of its open range, the lion of its kingship, the birds of their air?

I am no sentimentalist, God knows. I am in favor of vivisection unrestrained, so long as the vivisectionist knows what he is about. I advocate clubbing a dog that barks unnecessarily, which all dogs do. I enjoy hangings, particularly of converts to the evangelical faiths. The crunch of a cockroach is music to my ears. But when the day comes to turn the prisoners of the zoo out of their cages, if it is only to lead them to the swifter, kinder knife of the *schochet*, I shall be present and rejoicing, and if any one present thinks to suggest that it would be a good plan to celebrate the day by shooting the whole zoo faculty, I shall have a revolver in my pocket and a sound eye in my head.

XXXVII
ON HEARING MOZART

The only permanent values in the world are truth and beauty, and of these it is probable that truth is lasting only in so far as it is a function and manifestation of beauty—a projection of feeling in terms of idea. The world is a charnel house of dead religions. Where are all the faiths of the middle ages, so complex and yet so precise? But all that was essential in the beauty of the middle ages still lives . . .

This is the heritage of man, but not of men. The great majority of men are not even aware of it. Their participation in the progress of the world, and even in the history of the world, is infinitely remote and trivial. They live and die, at bottom, as animals live and die. The human race, as a race, is scarcely cognizant of their existence; they haven't even definite number, but stand grouped together as *x*, the quantity unknown . . . and not worth knowing.

XXXVIII
THE ROAD TO DOUBT

The first effect of what used to be called natural philosophy is to fill its devotee with wonder at the marvels of God. This explains why the pursuit of science, so long as it remains superficial, is not incompatible with the most naif sort of religious faith. But the moment the student of the sciences passes this stage of childlike amazement and begins to investigate the inner workings of natural phenomena, he begins to see how ineptly many of them are managed, and so he tends to pass from awe of the Creator to criticism of the Creator, and once he has crossed that bridge he has ceased to be a believer. One finds plenty of neighborhood physicians, amateur botanists, high-school physics teachers and other such quasi-scientists in the pews on Sunday, but one never sees a Huxley there, or a Darwin, or an Ehrlich.

XXXIX
A NEW USE FOR CHURCHES

The argument by design, it may be granted, establishes a reasonable ground for accepting the existence of God. It makes belief, at all events, quite as intelligible as unbelief. But when the theologians take their step from the existence of God to the goodness of God they tread upon much less firm earth. How can one see any proof of that goodness in the senseless and intolerable sufferings of man—his helplessness, the brief and troubled span of his life, the inexplicable disproportion between his deserts and his rewards, the tragedy of his soaring aspiration, the worse tragedy of his dumb questioning? Granting the existence of God, a house dedicated to Him naturally follows. He is all-important; it is fit that man should take some notice of Him. But why praise and flatter Him for His unspeakable cruelties? Why forget so supinely His failures to remedy the easily remediable? Why, indeed, devote the churches exclusively to worship? Why not give them over, now and then, to justifiable indignation meetings?

Perhaps men will incline to this idea later on. It is not inconceivable, indeed, that religion will one day cease to be a poltroonish acquiescence and become a vigorous and insistent criticism. If God can hear a petition, what ground is there for holding that He would not hear a complaint? It might, indeed, please Him to find His creatures grown so self-reliant and reflective. More, it might even help Him to get through His infinitely complex and difficult work. Theology has already moved toward such notions. It has abandoned the primitive doctrine of God's arbitrariness and indifference, and substituted the doctrine that He is willing, and even eager, to hear the desires of His creatures—*i. e.*, their private notions, born of experience, as to what would be best for them. Why assume that those notions would be any the less worth hearing and heeding if they were cast in the form of criticism, and even of denunciation? Why hold that the God who can understand and forgive even treason could not understand and forgive remonstrance?

XL
THE ROOT OF RELIGION

The idea of literal truth crept into religion relatively late: it is the invention of lawyers, priests and cheese-mongers. The idea of mystery long preceded it, and at the heart of that idea of mystery was an idea of beauty—that is, an idea that this or that view of the celestial and infernal process presented a satisfying picture of form, rhythm and organization. Once this view was adopted as satisfying, its professional interpreters and their dupes sought to reinforce it by declaring it true. The same flow of reasoning is familiar on lower planes. The average man does not get pleasure out of an idea because he thinks it is true; he thinks it is true because he gets pleasure out of it.

XLI
FREE WILL

Free will, it appears, is still a Christian dogma. Without it the cruelties of God would strain faith to the breaking-point. But outside the fold it is gradually falling into decay. Such men of science as George W. Crile and Jacques Loeb have dealt it staggering blows, and among laymen of inquiring mind it seems to be giving way to an apologetic sort of determinism—a determinism, one may say, tempered by defective observation. The late Mark Twain, in his secret heart, was such a determinist. In his "What Is Man?" you will find him at his farewells to libertarianism. The vast majority of our acts, he argues, are determined, but there remains a residuum of free choices. Here we stand free of compulsion and face a pair or more of alternatives, and are free to go this way or that.

A pillow for free will to fall upon—but one loaded with disconcerting brickbats. Where the occupants of this last trench of libertarianism err is in their assumption that the pulls of their antagonistic impulses are exactly equal—that the individual is absolutely free to choose which one he will yield to. Such freedom, in practise, is never encountered. When an individual confronts alternatives, it is not alone his volition that chooses between them, but also his environment, his inherited prejudices, his race, his color, his condition of servitude. I may kiss a girl or I may not kiss her, but surely it would be absurd to say that I am, in any true sense, a free agent in the matter. The world has even put my helplessness into a proverb. It says that my decision and act depend upon the time, the place—and even to some extent, upon the girl.

Examples might be multiplied *ad infinitum.* I can scarcely remember performing a wholly voluntary act. My whole life, as I look back upon it, seems to be a long series of inexplicable accidents, not only quite unavoidable, but even quite unintelligible. Its history is the history of the reactions of my personality to my environment, of my behavior before external stimuli. I have been no more responsible for that personality than I have been for that environment. To say that I can change the former by a voluntary effort is as ridiculous as to say that I can modify the curvature of the lenses of my eyes. I know, because I have often tried to change it, and always failed. Nevertheless, it has changed. I am not the same man I was in the last century. But the gratifying improvements so plainly visible are surely not to be credited to me. All of them came from without—or from unplumbable and uncontrollable depths within.

The more the matter is examined the more the residuum of free will shrinks and shrinks, until in the end it is almost impossible to find it. A great many men, of course, looking at themselves, see it as something very large; they slap their chests and call themselves free agents, and demand that God reward them for their virtue. But these fellows are simply idiotic egoists, devoid of a critical sense. They mistake the acts of God for their own acts. Of such sort are the coxcombs who boast about wooing and winning their wives. They are brothers to the fox who boasted that he had made the hounds run . . .

The throwing overboard of free will is commonly denounced on the ground that it subverts morality and makes of religion a mocking. Such pious objections, of course, are foreign to logic, but nevertheless it may be well to give a glance to this one. It is based upon the fallacious hypothesis that the determinist escapes, or hopes to escape, the consequences of his acts. Nothing could be more untrue. Consequences follow acts just as relentlessly if the latter be involuntary as if they be voluntary. If I rob a bank of my free choice or in response to some unfathomable inner necessity, it is all one; I will go to the same jail. Conscripts in war are killed just as often as volunteers. Men who are tracked down and shanghaied by their wives have just as hard a time of it as men who walk fatuously into the trap by formally proposing.

Even on the ghostly side, determinism does not do much damage to theology. It is no harder to believe that a man will be damned for his involuntary acts than it is to believe that he will be damned for his voluntary acts, for even the supposition that he is wholly free does not dispose of the massive fact that God made him as he is, and that God could have made him a saint if He had so desired. To deny this is to flout omnipotence—a crime at which, as I have often said, I balk. But here I begin to fear that I wade too far into the hot waters of the sacred sciences, and that I had better retire before I lose my hide. This prudent retirement is purely deterministic. I do not ascribe it to my own sagacity; I ascribe it wholly to that singular kindness which fate always shows me. If I were free I'd probably keep on, and then regret it afterward.

XLII
QUID EST VERITAS?

All great religions, in order to escape absurdity, have to admit a dilution of agnosticism. It is only the savage, whether of the African bush or the American gospel tent, who pretends to know the will and intent of God exactly and completely. "For who hath known the mind of the Lord?" asked Paul of the Romans. "How unsearchable are his judgments, and his ways past finding out!" "It is the glory of God," said Solomon, "to conceal a thing." "Clouds and darkness," said David, "are around him." "No man," said the Preacher, "can find out the work of God." . . . The difference between religions is a difference in their relative content of agnosticism. The most satisfying and ecstatic faith is almost purely agnostic. It trusts absolutely without professing to know at all.

XLIII
THE DOUBTER'S REWARD

Despite the common delusion to the contrary the philosophy of doubt is far more comforting than that of hope. The doubter escapes the worst penalty of the man of hope; he is never disappointed, and hence never indignant. The inexplicable and irremediable may interest him, but they do not enrage him, or, I may add, fool him. This immunity is worth all the dubious assurances ever foisted upon man. It is pragmatically impregnable . . . Moreover, it makes for tolerance and sympathy. The doubter does not hate his opponents; he sympathizes with them. In the end, he may even come to sympathize with God . . . The old idea of fatherhood here submerges in a new idea of brotherhood. God, too, is beset by limitations, difficulties, broken hopes. Is it disconcerting to think of Him thus? Well, is it any the less disconcerting to think of Him as able to ease and answer, and yet failing? . . .

But he that doubteth—*damnatus est.* At once the penalty of doubt—and its proof, excuse and genesis.

XLIV
BEFORE THE ALTAR

A salient objection to the prevailing religious ceremonial lies in the attitudes of abasement that it enforces upon the faithful. A man would be thought a slimy and knavish fellow if he approached any human judge or potentate in the manner provided for approaching the Lord God. It is an etiquette that involves loss of self-respect, and hence it cannot be pleasing to its object, for one cannot think of the Lord God as sacrificing decent feelings to mere vanity. This notion of abasement, like most of the other ideas that are general in the world, is obviously the invention of small and ignoble men. It is the pollution of theology by the *sklavmoral.*

XLV
THE MASK

Ritual is to religion what the music of an opera is to the libretto: ostensibly a means of interpretation, but actually a means of concealment. The Presbyterians made the mistake of keeping the doctrine of infant damnation in plain words. As enlightenment grew in the world, intelligence and prudery revolted against it, and so it had to be abandoned. Had it been set to music it would have survived—uncomprehended, unsuspected and unchallenged.

XLVI
PIA VENEZIANI, POI CRISTIANI

I have spoken of the possibility that God, too, may suffer from a finite intelligence, and so know the bitter sting of disappointment and defeat. Here I yielded something to politeness; the thing is not only possible, but obvious. Like man, God is deceived by appearances and probabilities; He makes calculations that do not work out; He falls into specious assumptions. For example, He assumed that Adam and Eve would obey the law in the Garden. Again, He assumed that the appalling lesson of the Flood would make men better. Yet again, He assumed that men would always put religion in first place among their concerns that it would be eternally possible to reach and influence them through it. This last assumption was the most erroneous of them all. The truth is that the generality of men have long since ceased to take religion seriously. When we encounter one who still does so, he seems eccentric, almost feeble-minded—or, more commonly, a rogue who has been deluded by his own hypocrisy. Even men who are professionally religious, and who thus have far more incentive to stick to religion than the rest of us, nearly always throw it overboard at the first serious temptation. During the past four years, for example, Christianity has been in combat with patriotism all over Christendom. Which has prevailed? How many gentlemen of God, having to choose between Christ and Patrie, have actually chosen Christ?

XLVII
OFF AGAIN, ON AGAIN

The ostensible object of the Reformation, which lately reached its fourth centenary, was to purge the Church of imbecilities. That object was accomplished; the Church shook them off. But imbecilities make an irresistible appeal to man; he inevitably tries to preserve them by cloaking them with religious sanctions. The result is Protestantism.

XLVIII
THEOLOGY

The notion that theology is a dull subject is one of the strangest delusions of a stupid and uncritical age. The truth is that some of the most engrossing books ever written in the world are full of it. For example, the Gospel according to St. Luke. For example, Nietzsche's "Der Antichrist." For example, Mark Twain's "What Is Man?", St. Augustine's Confessions, Haeckel's "The Riddle of the Universe," and Huxley's Essays. How, indeed, could a thing be dull that has sent hundreds of thousands of men—the very best and the very worst of the race—to the gallows and the stake, and made and broken dynasties, and inspired the greatest of human hopes and enterprises, and embroiled whole continents in war? No, theology is not a soporific. The reason it so often seems so is that its public exposition has chiefly fallen, in these later days, into the hands of a sect of intellectual castrati, who begin by mistaking it for a sub-department of etiquette, and then proceed to anoint it with butter, rose water and talcum powder. Whenever a first-rate intellect tackles it, as in the case of Huxley, or in that of Leo XIII., it at once takes on all the sinister fascination it had in Luther's day.

XLIX
EXEMPLI GRATIA

Do I let the poor suffer, and consign them, as old Friedrich used to say, to statistics and the devil? Well, so does God.

IN DEFENSE OF WOMEN

INTRODUCTION

As a professional critic of life and letters, my principal business in the world is that of manufacturing platitudes for tomorrow, which is to say, ideas so novel that they will be instantly rejected as insane and outrageous by all right thinking men, and so apposite and sound that they will eventually conquer that instinctive opposition, and force themselves into the traditional wisdom of the race. I hope I need not confess that a large part of my stock in trade consists of platitudes rescued from the cobwebbed shelves of yesterday, with new labels stuck rakishly upon them. This borrowing and refurbishing of shop-worn goods, as a matter of fact, is the invariable habit of traders in ideas, at all times and everywhere. It is not, however, that all the conceivable human notions have been thought out; it is simply, to be quite honest, that the sort of men who volunteer to think out new ones seldom, if ever, have wind enough for a full day's work. The most they can ever accomplish in the way of genuine originality is an occasional brilliant spurt, and half a dozen such spurts, particularly if they come close together and show a certain co-ordination, are enough to make a practitioner celebrated, and even immortal. Nature, indeed, conspires against all such genuine originality, and I have no doubt that God is against it on His heavenly throne, as His vicars and partisans unquestionably are on this earth. The dead hand pushes all of us into intellectual cages; there is in all of us a strange tendency to yield and have done. Thus the impertinent colleague of Aristotle is doubly beset, first by a public opinion that regards his enterprise as subversive and in bad taste, and secondly by an inner weakness that limits his capacity for it, and especially his capacity to throw off the prejudices and superstitions of his race, culture anytime. The cell, said Haeckel, does not act, it reacts—and what is the instrument of reflection and speculation save a congeries of cells? At the moment of the contemporary metaphysician's loftiest flight, when he is most gratefully warmed by the feeling that he is far above all the ordinary airlanes and has absolutely novel concept by the tail, he is suddenly pulled up by the discovery that what is entertaining him is simply the ghost of some ancient idea that his school-master forced into him in 1887, or the mouldering corpse of a doctrine that was made official in his country during the late war, or a sort of fermentation-product, to mix the figure, of a banal heresy launched upon him recently by his wife. This is the penalty that the man of intellectual curiosity and vanity pays for his violation of the divine edict that what has been revealed from Sinai shall suffice for him, and for his resistance to the natural process which seeks to reduce him to the respectable level of a patriot and taxpayer.

I was, of course, privy to this difficulty when I planned the present work, and entered upon it with no expectation that I should be able to embellish it with, almost, more than a very small number of hitherto unutilized notions. Moreover, I faced the additional handicap of having an audience of extraordinary antipathy to ideas before me, for I wrote it in war-time, with all foreign markets cut off, and so my only possible customers were Americans. Of their unprecedented dislike for novelty in the domain of the intellect I have often discoursed in the past, and so there is no need to go into the matter again. All I need do here is to recall the fact that, in the United States, alone among the great nations of history, there is a right way to think and a wrong way to think in everything—not only in theology, or politics, or economics, but in the most trivial matters of everyday life. Thus, in the average American city the citizen who, in the face of an organized public clamour(usually managed by interested parties) for the erection of an equestrian statue of Susan B. Anthony, the apostle of woman suffrage, in front of the chief railway station, or the purchase of a dozen leopards for the municipal zoo, or the dispatch of an invitation to the Structural Iron Workers' Union to hold its next annual convention in the town Symphony Hall—the citizen who, for any logical reason, opposes such a proposal—on the ground, say, that Miss Anthony never mounted a horse in her life, or that a dozen leopards would be less useful than a gallows to hang the City Council, or that the Structural Iron Workers would spit all over the floor of Symphony Hall and knock down the busts of Bach, Beethoven and Brahms—this citizen is commonly denounced as an anarchist and a public enemy. It is not only erroneous to think thus; it has come to be immoral. And many other planes, high and low. For an American to question any of the articles of fundamental faith cherished by the majority is for him to run grave risks of social disaster. The old English offence of "imagining the King's death" has been formally revived by the American courts, and hundreds of men and women are in jail for committing it, and it has been so enormously extended that, in some parts of the country at least, it now embraces such remote acts as believing that the negroes should have equality before the law, and speaking the language of countries recently at war with the Republic, and conveying to a private friend a formula for making synthetic gin. All such toyings with illicit ideas are construed as attentats against democracy, which, in a sense, perhaps they are. For democracy is grounded upon so childish a complex of fallacies that they must be protected by a rigid system of taboos, else even half-wits would argue it to pieces. Its first concern must thus be to penalize the free play of ideas. In the United States this is not only its first concern, but also its last concern. No other enterprise, not even the trade in public offices and contracts, occupies the rulers of the land so steadily, or makes heavier demands upon their ingenuity and their patriotic passion.

Familiar with the risks flowing out of it—and having just had to change the plates of my "Book of Prefaces," a book of purely literary criticism, wholly without political purpose or significance, in order to get it through the mails, I determined to make this brochure upon the woman question extremely pianissimo in tone, and to avoid burdening it with any ideas of an unfamiliar, and hence illegal nature. So deciding, I presently added a bravura touch: the unquenchable vanity of the intellectual snob asserting itself over all prudence. That is to say, I laid down the rule that no idea should go into the book that was not already so obvious that it had been embodied in the proverbial philosophy, or folk-wisdom, of some civilized nation, including the Chinese. To this rule I remained faithful throughout. In its original form, as published in 1918, the book was actuary just such a pastiche of proverbs, many of them English, and hence familiar even to Congressmen, newspaper editors and other such illiterates. It was not always easy to hold to this program; over and over again I was tempted to insert notions that seemed to have escaped the peasants of Europe and Asia. But in the end, at some cost to the form of the work, I managed to get through it without compromise, and so it was put into type. There is no need to add that my ideational abstinence went unrecognized and unrewarded. In fact, not a single American reviewer noticed it, and most of them slated the book violently as a mass of heresies and contumacies, a deliberate attack upon all the known and revered truths about the woman question, a headlong assault upon the national decencies. In the South, where the suspicion of ideas goes to extraordinary lengths, even for the United States, some of the newspapers actually denounced the book as German propaganda, designed to break down American morale, and called upon the Department of Justice to proceed against me for the crime known to American law as "criminal anarchy," i.e., "imagining the King's death." Why the Comstocks did not forbid it the mails as lewd and lascivious I have never been able to determine. Certainly, they received many complaints about it. I myself, in fact, caused a number of these complaints to be lodged, in the hope that the resultant buffooneries would give me entertainment in those dull days of war, with all intellectual activities adjourned, and maybe promote the sale of the book. But the Comstocks were pursuing larger fish, and so left me to the righteous indignation of right-thinking reviewers, especially the suffragists. Their concern, after all, is not with books that are denounced; what they concentrate their moral passion on is the book that is praised.

The present edition is addressed to a wider audience, in more civilized countries, and so I have felt free to introduce a number of propositions, not to be found in popular proverbs, that had to be omitted from the original edition. But even so, the book by no means pretends to preach revolutionary doctrines, or even doctrines of any novelty. All I design by it is to set down in more or less plain form certain ideas that practically every civilized man and woman holds in petto, but that have been concealed hitherto by the vast mass of sentimentalities swathing the whole woman question. It is a question of capital importance to all human beings, and it deserves to be discussed honestly and frankly, but there is so much of social reticence, of religious superstition and of mere emotion intermingled with it that most of the enormous literature it has thrown off is hollow and useless. I point for example, to the literature of the subsidiary question of woman suffrage. It fills whole libraries, but nine tenths of it is merely rubbish, for it starts off from assumptions that are obviously untrue and it reaches conclusions that are at war with both logic and the facts. So with the question of sex specifically. I have read, literally, hundreds of volumes upon it, and uncountable numbers of pamphlets, handbills and inflammatory wall-cards, and yet it leaves the primary problem unsolved, which is to say, the problem as to what is to be done about the conflict between the celibacy enforced upon millions by civilization and the appetites implanted in all by God. In the main, it counsels yielding to celibacy, which is exactly as sensible as advising a dog to forget its fleas. Here, as in other fields, I do not presume to offer a remedy of my own. In truth, I am very suspicious of all remedies for the major ills of life, and believe that most of them are incurable. But I at least venture todiscuss the matter realistically, and if what I have to say is not sagacious, it is at all events not evasive. This, I hope, is something. Maybe some later investigator will bring a better illumination to the subject.

It is the custom of The Free-Lance Series to print a paragraph or two about the author in each volume. I was born in Baltimore, September 12, 1880, and come of a learned family, though my immediate forebears were business men. The tradition of this ancient learning has been upon me since my earliest days, and I narrowly escaped becoming a doctor of philosophy. My father's death, in 1899, somehow dropped me into journalism, where I had a successful career, as such careers go. At the age of 25 1 was the chief editor of a daily newspaper in Baltimore. During the same year I published my first book of criticism. Thereafter, for ten or twelve years, I moved steadily from practical journalism, with its dabbles in politics, economics and soon, toward purely aesthetic concerns, chiefly literature and music, but of late I have felt a strong pull in the other direction, and what interests me chiefly today is what may be called public psychology, ie., the nature of the ideas that the larger masses of men hold, and the processes whereby they reach them. If I do any serious writing hereafter, it will be in that field. In the United States I am commonly held suspect as a foreigner, and during the war I was variously denounced. Abroad, especially in England, I am sometimes put to the torture for my intolerable Americanism. The two views are less far apart than they seem to be. The fact is that I am superficially so American, in ways of speech and thought, that the foreigner is deceived, whereas the native, more familiar with the true signs, sees that under the surface there is incurable antagonism to most of the ideas that Americans hold to be sound. Thus If all between two stools—but it is more comfortable there on the floor than sitting up tightly. I am wholly devoid of public spirit or moral purpose. This is incomprehensible to many men, and they seek to remedy the defect by crediting me with purposes of their own. The only thing I respect is intellectual honesty, of which, of course, intellectual courage is a necessary part. A Socialist who goes to jail for his opinions seems to me a much finer man than the judge who sends him there, though I disagree with all the ideas of the Socialist and agree with some of those of the judge. But though he is fine, the Socialist is nevertheless foolish, for he suffers for what is untrue. If I knew what was true, I'd probably be willing to sweat and strive for it, and maybe even to die for it to the tune of bugle-blasts. But so far I have not found it.

H. L. Mencken

I

The Feminine Mind

1.
The Maternal Instinct

A man's women folk, whatever their outward show of respect for his merit and authority, always regard him secretly as an ass, and with something akin to pity. His most gaudy sayings and doings seldom deceive them; they see the actual man within, and know him for a shallow and pathetic fellow. In this fact, perhaps, lies one of the best proofs of feminine intelligence, or, as the common phrase makes it, feminine intuition. The mark of that so-called intuition is simply a sharp and accurate perception of reality, an habitual immunity to emotional enchantment, a relentless capacity for distinguishing clearly between the appearance and the substance. The appearance, in the normal family circle, is a hero, magnifico, a demigod. The substance is a poor mountebank.

The proverb that no man is a hero to his valet is obviously of masculine manufacture. It is both insincere and untrue: insincere because it merely masks the egotistic doctrine that he is potentially a hero to everyone else, and untrue because a valet, being a fourth-rate man himself, is likely to be the last person in the world to penetrate his master's charlatanry. Who ever heard of valet who didn't envy his master wholeheartedly? who wouldn't willingly change places with his master? who didn't secretly wish that he was his master? A man's wife labours under no such naive folly. She may envy her husband, true enough, certain of his more soothing prerogatives and sentimentalities. She may envy him his masculine liberty of movement and occupation, his impenetrable complacency, his peasant-like delight in petty vices, his capacity for hiding the harsh face of reality behind the cloak of romanticism, his general innocence and childishness. But she never envies him his puerile ego; she never envies him his shoddy and preposterous soul.

This shrewd perception of masculine bombast and make-believe, this acute understanding of man as the eternal tragic comedian, is at the bottom of that compassionate irony which paces under the name of the maternal instinct. A woman wishes to mother a man simply because she sees into his helplessness, his need of an amiable environment, his touching self delusion. That ironical note is not only daily apparent in real life; it sets the whole tone of feminine fiction. The woman novelist, if she be skillful enough to arise out of mere imitation into genuine self-expression, never takes her heroes quite seriously. From the day of George Sand to the day of Selma Lagerlof she has always got into her character study a touch of superior aloofness, of ill-concealed derision. I can't recall a single masculine figure created by a woman who is not, at bottom, a booby.

2.
Women's Intelligence

That is should still be necessary, at this late stage in the senility of the human race to argue that women have a fine and fluent intelligence is surely an eloquent proof of the defective observation, incurable prejudice, and general imbecility of their lords and masters. One finds very few professors of the subject, even among admitted feminists, approaching the fact as obvious; practically all of them think it necessary to bring up a vast mass of evidence to establish what should be an axiom. Even the Franco Englishman, W. L. George, one of the most sharp-witted of the faculty, wastes a whole book up on the demonstration, and then, with a great air of uttering something new, gives it the humourless title of "The Intelligence of Women. "The intelligence of women, forsooth! As well devote a laborious time to the sagacity of serpents, pickpockets, or Holy Church!

Women, in truth, are not only intelligent; they have almost a monopoly of certain of the subtler and more utile forms of intelligence. The thing itself, indeed, might be reasonably described as a special feminine character; there is in it, in more than one of its manifestations, a femaleness as palpable as the femaleness of cruelty, masochism or rouge. Men are strong. Men are brave in physical combat. Men have sentiment. Men are romantic, and love what they conceive to be virtue and beauty. Men incline to faith, hope and charity. Men know how to sweat and endure. Men are amiable and fond. But in so far as they show the true fundamentals of intelligence—in so far as they reveal a capacity for discovering the kernel of eternal verity in the husk of delusion and hallucination and a passion for bringing it forth—to that extent, at least, they are feminine, and still nourished by the milk of their mothers. "Human creatures," says George, borrowing from Weininger, "are never entirely male or entirely female; there are no men, there are no women, but only sexual majorities." Find me an obviously intelligent man, a man free from sentimentality and illusion, a man hard to deceive, a man of the first class, and I'll show you aman with a wide streak of woman in him. Bonaparte had it; Goethe had it; Schopenhauer had it; Bismarck and Lincoln had it; in Shakespeare, if the Freudians are to be believed, it amounted to down right homosexuality. The essential traits and qualities of the male, the hallmarks of the unpolluted masculine, are at the same time the hallmarks of the Schalskopf. The caveman is all muscles and mush. Without a woman to rule him and think for him, he is a truly lamentable spectacle: a baby with whiskers, a rabbit with the frame of an aurochs, a feeble and preposterous caricature of God.

It would be an easy matter, indeed, to demonstrate that superior talent in man is practically always accompanied by this feminine flavour—that complete masculinity and stupidity are often indistinguishable. Lest I be misunderstood I hasten to add that I do not mean to say that masculinity contributes nothing to the complex of chemico-physiological reactions which produces what we call talent; all I mean to say is that this complex is impossible without the feminine contribution that it is a product of the interplay of the two elements. In women of genius we see the opposite picture. They are commonly distinctly mannish, and shave as well as shine. Think of George Sand, Catherine the Great, Elizabeth of England, Rosa Bonheur, Teresa Carreo or Cosima Wagner. The truth is that neither sex, without some fertilization by the complementary characters of the other, is capable of the highest reaches of human endeavour. Man, without a saving touch of woman in him, is too doltish, too naive and romantic, too easily deluded and lulled to sleep by his imagination to be anything above a cavalryman, a theologian or a bank director. And woman, without some trace of that divine innocence which is masculine, is too harshly the realist for those vast projections of the fancy which lie at the heart of what we call genius. Here, as elsewhere in the universe, the best effects are obtained by a mingling of elements. The wholly manly man lacks the wit necessary to give objective form to his soaring and secret dreams, and the wholly womanly woman is apt to be too cynical a creature to dream at all.

3.

The Masculine Bag of Tricks

What men, in their egoism, constantly mistake for a deficiency of intelligence in woman is merely an incapacity for mastering that mass of small intellectual tricks, that complex of petty knowledges, that collection of cerebral rubber stamps, which constitutes the chief mental equipment of the average male. A man thinks that he is more intelligent than his wife because he can add up a column of figures more accurately, and because he understands the imbecile jargon of the stock market, and because he is able to distinguish between the ideas of rival politicians, and because he is privy to the minutiae of some sordid and degrading business or profession, say soap-selling or the law. But these empty talents, of course, are not really signs of a profound intelligence; they are, in fact, merely superficial accomplishments, and their acquirement puts little more strain on the mental powers than a chimpanzee suffers in learning how to catch a penny or scratch a match. The whole bag of tricks of the average business man, or even of the average professional man, is inordinately childish. It takes no more actual sagacity to carry on the everyday hawking and haggling of the world, or to ladle out its normal doses of bad medicine and worse law, than intakes to operate a taxicab or fry a pan of fish. No observant person, indeed, can come into close contact with the general run of business and professional men—I confine myself to those who seem to get on in the world, and exclude the admitted failures—without marvelling at their intellectual lethargy, their incurable ingenuousness, their appalling lack of ordinary sense. The late Charles Francis Adams, a grandson of one American President and a great-grandson of another, after a long lifetime in intimate association with some of the chief business "geniuses" of that paradise of traders and usurers, the United States, reported in his old age that he had never heard a single one of them say anything worth hearing. These were vigorous and masculine men, and in a man's world they were successful men, but intellectually they were all blank cartridges.

There is, indeed, fair ground for arguing that, if men of that kidney were genuinely intelligent, they would never succeed at their gross an driveling concerns—that their very capacity to master and retain such balderdash as constitutes their stock in trade is proof of their inferior mentality. The notion is certainly supported by the familiar incompetency of first rate men for what are called practical concerns. One could not think of Aristotle or Beethoven multiplying 3,472,701 by 99,999 without making a mistake, nor could one think of him remembering the range of this or that railway share for two years, or the number of ten-penny nails in a hundred weight, or the freight on lard from Galveston to Rotterdam. And by the same token one could not imagine him expert at billiards, or at grouse-shooting, or at golf, or at any other of the idiotic games at which what are called successful men commonly divert themselves. In his great study of British genius, Havelock Ellis found that an incapacity for such petty expertness was visible in almost all first rate men. They are bad at tying cravats. They do not understand the fashionable card games. They are puzzled by book-keeping. They know nothing of party politics. In brief, they are inert and impotent in the very fields of endeavour that see the average men's highest performances, and are easily surpassed by men who, in actual intelligence, are about as far below them as the Simidae.

This lack of skill at manual and mental tricks of a trivial character—which must inevitably appear to a barber or a dentist as stupidity, and to a successful haberdasher as downright imbecility—is a character that men of the first class share with women of the first, second and even third classes. There is at the bottom of it, in truth, something unmistakably feminine; its appearance in a man is almost invariably accompanied by the other touch of femaleness that I have described. Nothing, indeed, could be plainer than the fact that women, as a class, are sadly deficient in the small expertness of men as a class. One seldom, if ever, hears of them succeeding in the occupations which bring out such expertness most lavishly—for example, tuning pianos, repairing clocks, practising law, (ie., matching petty tricks with some other lawyer), painting portraits, keeping books, or managing factories—despite the circumstance that the great majority of such occupations are well within their physical powers, and that few of them offer any very formidable social barriers to female entrance. There is no external reason why women shouldn't succeed as operative surgeons; the way is wide open, the rewards are large, and there is a special demand for them on grounds of modesty. Nevertheless, not many women graduates in medicine undertake surgery and it is rare for one of them to make a success of it. There is, again, no external reason why women should not prosper at the bar, or as editors of newspapers, or as managers of the lesser sort of factories, or in the wholesale trade, or as hotel-keepers. The taboos that stand in the way are of very small force; various adventurous women have defied them with impunity; once the door is entered there remains no special handicap within. But, as every one knows, the number of women actually practising these trades and professions is very small, and few of them have attained to any distinction in competition with men.

4.

Why Women Fail

The cause thereof, as I say, is not external, but internal. It lies in the same disconcerting apprehension of the larger realities, the same impatience with the paltry and meretricious, the same disqualification for mechanical routine and empty technic which one finds in the higher varieties of men. Even in the pursuits which, by the custom of Christendom, are especially their own, women seldom show any of that elaborately conventionalized and half automatic proficiency which is the pride and boast of most men. It is a commonplace of observation, indeed, that a housewife who actually knows how to cook, or who can make her own clothes with enough skill to conceal the fact from the most casual glance, or who is competent to instruct her children in the elements of morals, learning and hygiene—it is a platitude that such a woman is very rare indeed, and that when she is encountered she is not usually esteemed for her general intelligence. This is particularly true in the United States, where the position of women is higher than in any other civilized or semi-civilized country, and the old assumption of their intellectual inferiority has been most successfully challenged. The American dinner-table, in truth, becomes a monument to the defective technic of the American housewife. The guest who respects his oesophagus, invited to feed upon its discordant and ill-prepared victuals, evades the experience as long and as often as he can, and resigns himself toit as he might resign himself to being shaved by a paralytic. Nowhere else in the world have women more leisure and freedom to improve their minds, and nowhere else do they show a higher level of intelligence, or take part more effectively in affairs of the first importance. But nowhere else is there worse cooking in the home, or a more inept handling of the whole domestic economy, or a larger dependence upon the aid of external substitutes, by men provided, for the skill that wanting where it theoretically exists. It is surely no mere coincidence that the land of the emancipated and enthroned woman is also the land of canned soup, of canned pork and beans, of whole meals in cans, and of everything else ready-made. And nowhere else is there more striking tendency to throw the whole business of training the minds of children upon professional teachers, and the whole business of instructing them in morals and religion upon so-called Sunday-schools, and the whole business of developing and caring for their bodies upon playground experts, sex hygienists and other such professionals, most of them mountebanks.

In brief, women rebel—often unconsciously, sometimes even submitting all the while—against the dull, mechanical tricks of the trade that the present organization of society compels them to practise for a living, and that rebellion testifies to their intelligence. If they enjoyed and took pride in those tricks, and showed it by diligence and skill, they would be on all fours with such men as are headwaiters, ladies' tailors, schoolmasters or carpet-beaters, and proud of it. The inherent tendency of any woman above the most stupid is to evade the whole obligation, and, if she cannot actually evade it, to reduce its demands to the minimum. And when some accident purges her, either temporarily or permanently, of the inclination to marriage (of which much more anon), and she enters into competition with men in the general business of the world, the sort of career that she commonly carves out offers additional evidence of her mental peculiarity. In whatever calls for no more than an invariable technic and a feeble chicanery she usually fails; in whatever calls for independent thought and resourcefulness she usually succeeds. Thus she is almost always a failure as a lawyer, for the law requires only an armament of hollow phrases and stereotyped formulae, and a mental habit which puts these phantasms above sense, truth and justice; and she is almost always a failure in business, for business, in the main, is so foul a compound of trivialities and rogueries that her sense of intellectual integrity revolts against it. But she is usually a success as a sick-nurse, for that profession requires ingenuity, quick comprehension, courage in the face of novel and disconcerting situations, and above all, a capacity for penetrating and dominating character; and whenever she comes into competition with men in the arts, particularly on those secondary planes where simple nimbleness of mind is unaided by the masterstrokes of genius, she holds her own invariably. The best and most intellectual—i.e., most original and enterprising play-actors are not men, but women, and so are the best teachers and blackmailers, and a fair share of the best writers, and public functionaries, and executants of music. In the demimonde one will find enough acumen and daring, and enough resilience in the face of special difficulties, to put the equipment of any exclusively male profession to shame. If the work of the average man required half the mental agility and readiness of resource of the work of the average prostitute, the average man would be constantly on the verge of starvation.

5.

The Thing Called Intuition

Men, as every one knows, are disposed to question this superior intelligence of women; their egoism demands the denial, and they are seldom reflective enough to dispose of it by logical and evidential analysis. Moreover, as we shall see a bit later on, there is a certain specious appearance of soundness in their position; they have forced upon women an artificial character which well conceals their real character, and women have found it profitable to encourage the deception. But though every normal man thus cherishes the soothing unction that he is the intellectual superior of all women, and particularly of his wife, he constantly gives the lie to his pretension by consulting and deferring to what he calls her intuition. That is to say, he knows by experience that her judgment in many matters of capital concern is more subtle and searching than his own, and, being disinclined to accredit this greater sagacity to a more competent intelligence, he takes refuge behind the doctrine that it is due to some impenetrable and intangible talent for guessing correctly, some half mystical super sense, some vague(and, in essence, infra-human) instinct.

The true nature of this alleged instinct, however, is revealed by an examination of the situations which inspire a man to call it to his aid. These situations do not arise out of the purely technical problems that are his daily concern, but out of the rarer and more fundamental, and hence enormously more difficult problems which beset him only at long and irregular intervals, and go offer a test, not of his mere capacity for being drilled, but of his capacity for genuine ratiocination. No man, I take it, save one consciously inferior and hen-pecked, would consult his wife about hiring a clerk, or about extending credit to some paltry customer, or about some routine piece of tawdry swindling; but not even the most egoistic man would fail to sound the sentiment of his wife about taking a partner into his business, or about standing for public office, or about combating unfair and ruinous competition, or about marrying off their daughter. Such things are of massive importance; they lie at the foundation of well-being; they call for the best thought that the, man confronted by them can muster; the perils hidden in a wrong decision overcome even the clamors of vanity. It is in such situations that the superior mental grasp of women is of obvious utility, and has to be admitted. It is here that they rise above the insignificant sentimentalities, superstitions and formulae of men, and apply to the business their singular talent for separating the appearance from the substance, and so exercise what is called their intuition.

Intuition? With all respect, bosh! Then it was intuition that led Darwin to work out the hypothesis of natural selection. Then it was intuition that fabricated the gigantically complex score of "Die Walkure." Then it was intuition that convinced Columbus of the existence of land to the west of the Azores. All this intuition of which so much transcendental rubbish is merchanted is no more and no less than intelligence—intelligence so keen that it can penetrate to the hidden truth through the most formidable wrappings of false semblance and demeanour, and so little corrupted by sentimental prudery that it is equal to the even more difficult task of hauling that truth out into the light, in all its naked hideousness. Women decide the larger questions of life correctly and quickly, not because they are lucky guessers, not because they are divinely inspired, not because they practise a magic inherited from savagery, but simply and solely because they have sense. They see at a glance what most men could not see with searchlights and telescopes; they are at grips with the essentials of a problem before men have finished debating its mere externals. They are the supreme realists of the race. Apparently illogical, they are the possessors of a rare and subtle super-logic. Apparently whimsical, they hang to the truth with a tenacity which carries them through every phase of its incessant, jellylike shifting of form. Apparently unobservant and easily deceived, they see with bright and horrible eyes. In men, too, the same merciless perspicacity sometimes shows itself—men recognized to be more aloof and uninflammable than the general—men of special talent for the logical—sardonic men, cynics. Men, too, sometimes have brains. But that is a rare, rare man, I venture, who is as steadily intelligent, as constantly sound in judgment, as little put off by appearances, as the average women of forty-eight.

II

The War Between the Sexes

6.
How Marriages are Arranged

I have said that women are not sentimental, i.e., not prone to permit mere emotion and illusion to corrupt their estimation of a situation. The doctrine, perhaps, will raise a protest. The theory that they are is itself a favourite sentimentality; one sentimentality will be brought up to substantiate another; dog will eat dog. But an appeal to a few obvious facts will be enough to sustain my contention, despite the vast accumulation of romantic rubbish to the contrary.

Turn, for example, to the field in which the two sexes come most constantly into conflict, and in which, as a result, their habits of mind are most clearly contrasted—to the field, to wit, of monogamous marriage. Surely no long argument is needed to demonstrate the superior competence and effectiveness of women here, and therewith their greater self-possession, their saner weighing of considerations, their higher power of resisting emotional suggestion. The very fact that marriages occur at all is a proof, indeed, that they are more cool-headed than men, and more adept in employing their intellectual resources, for it is plainly to a man's interest to avoid marriage as long as possible, and as plainly to a woman's interest to make a favourable marriage as soon as she can. The efforts of the two sexes are thus directed, in one of the capital concerns of life, to diametrically antagonistic ends. Which side commonly prevails? I leave the verdict to the jury. All normal men fight the thing off; some men are successful for relatively long periods; a few extraordinarily intelligent and courageous men (or perhaps lucky ones) escape altogether. But, taking one generation with another, as every one knows, the average man is duly married and the average woman gets a husband. Thus the great majority of women, in this clear-cut and endless conflict, make manifest their substantial superiority to the great majority of men.

Not many men, worthy of the name, gain anything of net value by marriage, at least as the [institution is now met with in Christendom. Even assessing its benefits at their most inflated worth, they are plainly overborne by crushing disadvantages. When a man marries it is no more than a sign that the feminine talent for persuasion and intimidation—i.e., the feminine talent for survival in a world of clashing concepts and desires, the feminine competence and intelligence—has forced him into a more or less abhorrent compromise with his own honest inclinations and best interests. Whether that compromise be a sign of his relative stupidity or of his relative cowardice it is all one: the two things, in their symptoms and effects, are almost identical. In the first case he marries because he has been clearly bowled over in a combat of wits; in the second he resigns himself to marriage as the safest form of liaison. In both cases his inherent sentimentality is the chief weapon in the hand of his opponent. It makes him [caroche] the fiction of his enterprise, and even of his daring, in the midst of the most crude and obvious operations against him. It makes him accept as real the bold play-acting that women always excel at, and at no time more than when stalking a man. It makes him, above all, see a glamour of romance in a transaction which, even at its best, contains almost as much gross trafficking, at bottom, as the sale of a mule.

A man in full possession of the modest faculties that nature commonly apportions to him is at least far enough above idiocy to realize that marriages a bargain in which he gets the worse of it, even when, in some detail or other, he makes a visible gain. He never, I believe, wants all that the thing offers and implies. He wants, at most, no more than certain parts. He may desire, let us say, a housekeeper to protect his goods and entertain his friends—but he may shrink from the thought of sharing his bathtub with anyone, and home cooking may be downright poisonous to him. He may yearn for a son to pray at his tomb—and yet suffer acutely at the me reapproach of relatives-in-law. He may dream of a beautiful and complaisant mistress, less exigent and mercurial than any a bachelor may hope to discover—and stand aghast at admitting her to his bank-book, his family-tree and his secret ambitions. He may want company and not intimacy, or intimacy and not company. He may want a cook and not a partner in his business, or a partner in his business and not a cook. But in order to get the precise thing or things that he wants, he has to take a lot of other things that he doesn't want—that no sane man, in truth, could imaginably want—and it is to the enterprise of forcing him into this almost Armenian bargain that the woman of his "choice" addresses herself. Once the game is fairly set, she searches out his weaknesses with the utmost delicacy and accuracy, and plays upon them with all her superior resources. He carries a handicap from the start. His sentimental and unintelligent belief in theories that she knows quite well are not true—e.g., the theory that she shrinks from him, and is modestly appalled by the banal carnalities of marriage itself—gives her a weapon against him which she drives home with instinctive and compelling art. The moment she discerns this sentimentality bubbling within him—that is, The moment his oafish smirks and eye rollings signify that he has achieved the intellectual disaster that is called falling in love—he is hers to do with as she will. Save for acts of God, he is forthwith as good as married.

7.

The Feminine Attitude

This sentimentality in marriage is seldom, if ever, observed in women. For reasons that we shall examine later, they have much more to gain by the business than men, and so they are prompted by their cooler sagacity tenter upon it on the most favourable terms possible, and with the minimum admixture of disarming emotion. Men almost invariably get their mates by the process called falling in love; save among the aristocracies of the North and Latin men, the marriage of convenience is relatively rare; a hundred men marry "beneath" them to every woman who perpetrates the same folly. And what is meant by this so-called falling in love? What is meant by it is a procedure whereby a man accounts for the fact of his marriage, after feminine initiative and generalship have made it inevitable, by enshrouding it in a purple maze of romance—in brief, by setting up the doctrine that an obviously self-possessed and mammalian woman, engaged deliberately in the most important adventure of her life, and with the keenest understanding of its utmost implications, is a naive, tender, moony and almost disembodied creature, enchanted and made perfect by a passion that has stolen upon her unawares, and which she could not acknowledge, even to herself, without blushing to death. By this preposterous doctrine, the defeat and enslavement of the man is made glorious, and even gifted with a touch of flattering naughtiness. The sheer horsepower of his wooing has assailed and overcome her maiden modesty; she trembles in his arms; he has been granted a free franchise to work his wicked will upon her. Thus do the ambulant images of God cloak their shackles proudly, and divert the judicious with their boastful shouts.

Women, it is almost needless to point out, are much more cautious about embracing the conventional hocus-pocus of the situation. They never acknowledge that they have fallen in love, as the phrase is, until the man has formally avowed the delusion, and so cut off his retreat; to do otherwise would be to bring down upon their heads the mocking and contumely of all their sisters. With them, falling in love thus appears in the light of an afterthought, or, perhaps more accurately, in the light of a contagion. The theory, it would seem, is that the love of the man, laboriously avowed, has inspired it instantly, and by some unintelligible magic; that it was non-existent until the heat of his own flames set it off. This theory, it must be acknowledged, has a certain element of fact in it. A woman seldom allows herself to be swayed by emotion while the principal business is yet afoot and its issue still in doubt; to do so would be to expose a degree of imbecility that is confined only to the half-wits of the sex. But once the man is definitely committed, she frequently unbends a bit, if only as a relief from the strain of a fixed purpose, and so, throwing off her customary inhibitions, she, indulges in the luxury of a more or less forced and mawkish sentiment. It is, however, almost unheard of for her to permit herself this relaxation before the sentimental intoxication of the man is assured. To do otherwise—that is, to confess, even post facto, to an anterior descent,—would expose her, as I have said, to the scorn of all other women. Such a confession would be an admission that emotion had got the better of her at a critical intellectual moment, and in the eyes of women, as in the eyes of the small minority of genuinely intelligent men, no treason to the higher cerebral centres could be more disgraceful.

8.

The Male Beauty

This disdain of sentimental weakness, even in those higher reaches where it is mellowed by aesthetic sensibility, is well revealed by the fact that women are seldom bemused by mere beauty in men. Save on the stage, the handsome fellow has no appreciable advantage in amour over his more Gothic brother. In real life, indeed, he is viewed with the utmost suspicion by all women save the most stupid. In him the vanity native to his sex is seen to mount to a degree that is positively intolerable. It not only irritates by its very nature; it also throws about him a sort of unnatural armour, and so makes him resistant to the ordinary approaches. For this reason, the matrimonial enterprises of the more reflective and analytical sort of women are almost always directed to men whose lack of pulchritude makes them easier to bring down, and, what is more important still, easier to hold down. The weight of opinion among women is decidedly against the woman who falls in love with an Apollo. She is regarded, at best, as flighty creature, and at worst, as one pushing bad taste to the verge of indecency. Such weaknesses are resigned to women approaching senility, and to the more ignoble variety of women labourers. A shop girl, perhaps, may plausibly fall in love with a moving-picture actor, and a half-idiotic old widow may succumb to a youth with shoulders like the Parthenon, but no woman of poise and self-respect, even supposing her to be transiently flustered by a lovely buck, would yield to that madness for an instant, or confess it to her dearest friend. Women know how little such purely superficial values are worth. The voice of their order, the first taboo of their freemasonry, is firmly against making a sentimental debauch of the serious business of marriage.

This disdain of the pretty fellow is often accounted for by amateur psychologists on the ground that women are anesthetic to beauty—that they lack the quick and delicate responsiveness of man. Nothing could be more absurd. Women, in point of fact, commonly have a far keener aesthetic sense than men. Beauty is more important to them; they give more thought to it; they crave more of it in their immediate surroundings. The average man, at least in England and America, takes a sort of bovine pride in his anaesthesia to the arts; he can think of them only as sources of tawdry and somewhat discreditable amusement; one seldom hears of him showing half the enthusiasm for any beautiful thing that his wife displays in the presence, of a fine fabric, an effective colour, or a graceful form, say in millinery. The, truth is that women are resistant to so-called beauty in men for the simple and sufficient reason that such beauty is chiefly imaginary. A truly beautiful man, indeed, is as rare as a truly beautiful piece of jewelry. What men mistake for beauty in themselves is usually nothing save a certain hollow gaudiness, a revolting flashiness, the superficial splendour of a prancing animal. The most lovely moving picture actor, considered in the light of genuine aesthetic values, is no more than a piece of vulgarity; his like is to be found, not in the Uffizi gallery or among the harmonies of Brahms, but among the plush sofas, rococo clocks and hand-painted oil-paintings of a third-rate auction room. All women, save the least intelligent, penetrate this imposture with sharp eyes. They know that the human body, except for a brief time in infancy, is not a beautiful thing, buta hideous thing. Their own bodies give them no delight; it is their constant effort to disguise and conceal them; they never expose them aesthetically, but only as an act of the grossest sexual provocation. If it were advertised that a troupe of men of easy virtue were to appear half-clothed upon a public stage, exposing their chests, thighs, arms and calves, the only women who would go to the entertainment would be a few delayed adolescents, a psychopathic old maid or two, and a guard of indignant members of the parish Ladies Aid Society.

9.

Men as Aesthetes

Men show no such sagacious apprehension of the relatively feeble loveliness of the human frame. The most effective lure that a woman can hold out to a man is the lure of what he fatuously conceives to be her beauty. This so-called beauty, of course, is almost always a pure illusion. The female body, even at its best is very defective in form; it has harsh curves and very clumsily distributed masses; compared to it the average milk-jug, or even cuspidor, is a thing of intelligent and gratifying design—in brief, an objet d'art. The fact was curiously (and humorously) display during the late war, when great numbers of women in all the belligerent countries began putting on uniforms. Instantly they appeared in public in their grotesque burlesques of the official garb of aviators, elevator boys, bus conductors, train guards, and so on, their deplorable deficiency in design was unescapably revealed. A man, save he be fat, i.e., of womanish contours, usually looks better in uniform than in mufti; the tight lines set off his figure. But a woman is at once given away: she look like a dumbbell run over by an express train. Below the neck by the bow and below the waist astern there are two masses that simply refuse to fit into a balanced composition. Viewed from the side, she presents an exaggerated S bisected by an imperfect straight line, and so she inevitably suggests a drunken dollar-mark. Her ordinary clothing cunningly conceals this fundamental imperfection. It swathes those impossible masses in draperies soothingly uncertain of outline. But putting her into uniform is like stripping her. Instantly all her alleged beauty vanishes.

Moreover, it is extremely rare to find a woman who shows even the modest sightliness that her sex is theoretically capable of; it is only the rare beauty who is even tolerable. The average woman, until art comes to her aid, is ungraceful, misshapen, badly calved and crudely articulated, even for a woman. If she has a good torso, she is almost sure to be bow-legged. If she has good legs, she is almost sure to have bad teeth. If she has good teeth, she is almost sure to have scrawny hands, or muddy eyes, or hair like oakum, or no chin. A woman who meets fair tests all 'round is so uncommon that she becomes a sort of marvel, and usually gains a livelihood by exhibiting herself as such, either on the stage, in the half-world, or as the private jewel of some wealthy connoisseur.

But this lack of genuine beauty in women lays on them no practical disadvantage in the primary business of their sex, for its effects are more than overborne by the emotional suggestibility, the herculean capacity for illusion, the almost total absence of critical sense of men. Men do not demand genuine beauty, even in the most modest doses; they are quite content with the mere appearance of beauty. That is to say, they show no talent whatever for differentiating between the artificial and the real. A film of face powder, skilfully applied, is as satisfying to them as an epidermis of damask. The hair of a dead Chinaman, artfully dressed and dyed, gives them as much delight as the authentic tresses of Venus.

A false hip intrigues them as effectively as the soundest one of living fascia. A pretty frock fetches them quite as surely and securely as lovely legs, shoulders, hands or eyes. In brief, they estimate women, and hence acquire their wives, by reckoning up purely superficial aspects, which is just as intelligent as estimating an egg by purely superficial aspects. They never go behind the returns; it never occurs to them to analyze the impressions they receive. The result is that many a man, deceived by such paltry sophistications, never really sees his wife—that if, as God is supposed to see, her, and as the embalmer will see her—until they have been married for years. All the tricks may be infantile and obvious, but in the face of so naive a spectator the temptation to continue practising them is irresistible. A trained nurse tells me that even when undergoing the extreme discomforts of parturition the great majority of women continue to modify their complexions with pulverized talcs, and to give thought to the arrangement of their hair. Such transparent devices, to be sure, reduce the psychologist to a sour sort of mirth, and yet it must be plain that they suffice to entrap and make fools of men, even the most discreet. I know of no man, indeed, who is wholly resistant to female beauty, and I know of no man, even among those engaged professionally by aesthetic problems, who habitually and automatically distinguishes the genuine, from the imitation. He may doit now and then; he may even preen himself upon is on unusual discrimination; but given the right woman and the right stage setting, and he will be deceived almost as readily as a yokel fresh from the cabbage-field.

10.

The Process of Delusion

Such poor fools, rolling their eyes in appraisement of such meagre female beauty as is on display in Christendom, bring to their judgments a capacity but slightly greater than that a cow would bring to the estimation of epistemologies. They are so unfitted for the business that they are even unable to agree upon its elements. Let one such man succumb to the plaster charms of some. prancing miss, and all his friends will wonder what is the matter with him. No two are in accord as to which is the most beautiful woman in their own town or street. Turn six of them loose in millinery shop or the parlour of a bordello, and there will be no dispute whatsoever; each will offer the crown of love and beauty to a different girl.

And what aesthetic deafness, dumbness and blindness thus open the way for, vanity instantly reinforces. That is to say, once a normal man has succumbed to the meretricious charms of a definite fair one (or, more accurately, once a definite fair one has marked him out and grabbed him by the nose), he defends his choice with all the heat and steadfastness appertaining to the defense of a point of the deepest honour. To tell a man flatly that his wife is not beautiful, or even that his stenographer or manicurist is not beautiful, is so harsh and intolerable an insult to his taste that even an enemy seldom ventures upon it. One would offend him far less by arguing that his wife is an idiot. One would relatively speaking, almost caress him by spitting into his eye. The ego of the male is simply unable to stomach such an affront. It is a weapon as discreditable as the poison of the Borgias.

Thus, on humane grounds, a conspiracy of silence surrounds the delusion of female beauty, and so its victim is permitted to get quite as much delight out of it as if it were sound. The baits he swallows most are not edible and nourishing baits, but simply bright and gaudy ones. He succumbs to a pair of well-managed eyes, a graceful twist of the body, a synthetic complexion or a skilful display of ankles without giving the slightest thought to the fact that a whole woman is there, and that within the cranial cavity of the woman lies a brain, and that the idiosyncrasies of that brain are of vastly more importance than all imaginable physical stigmata combined. Those idiosyncrasies may make for amicable relations in the complex and difficult bondage called marriage; they may, on the contrary, make for joustings of a downright impossible character. But not many men, laced] in the emotional maze preceding, are capable of any very clear examination of such facts. The truth is that they dodge the facts, even when they are favourable, and lay all stress upon the surrounding and concealing superficialities. The average stupid and sentimental man, if he has a noticeably sensible wife, is almost apologetic about it. The ideal of his sex is always a pretty wife, and the vanity and coquetry that so often go with prettiness are erected into charms. In other words, men play the love game so unintelligently that they often esteem a woman in proportion as she seems to disdain and make a mock of her intelligence. Women seldom, if ever, make that blunder. What they commonly value in a man is not mere showiness, whether physical or spiritual, but that compound of small capacities which makes up masculine efficiency and passes for masculine intelligence. This intelligence, at its highest, has a human value substantially equal to that of their own. In a man's world it at least gets its definite rewards; it guarantees security, position, a livelihood; it is a commodity that is merchantable. Women thus accord it a certain respect, and esteem it in their husbands, and so seek it out.

11.

Biological Considerations

So far as I can make out by experiments on laboratory animals and by such discreet vivisections as are possible under our laws, there is no biological necessity for the superior acumen and circumspection of women. That is to say, it does not lie in any anatomical or physiological advantage. The essential feminine machine is no better than the essential masculine machine; both are monuments to the maladroitness of a much over-praised Creator. Women, it would seem, actually have smaller brains than men, though perhaps not in proportion to weight. Their nervous responses, if anything, are a bit duller than those of men; their muscular coordinations are surely no prompter. One finds quite as many obvious botches among them; they have as many bodily blemishes; they are infested by the same microscopic parasites; their senses are as obtuse; their ears stand out as absurdly. Even assuming that their special malaises are wholly offset by the effects of alcoholism in the male, they suffer patently from the same adenoids, gastritis, cholelithiasis, nephritis, tuberculosis, carcinoma, arthritis and so on—in short, from the same disturbances of colloidal equilibrium that produce religion, delusions of grandeur, democracy, pyaemia, night sweats, the yearning to save humanity, and all other such distempers in men. They have, at bottom, the same weaknesses and appetites. They react in substantially the same way to all chemical and mechanical agents. A dose of hydrocyanic acid, administered per ora to the most sagacious woman imaginable, affects her just as swiftly and just as deleteriously as it affects a tragedian, a crossing-sweeper, or an ambassador to the Court of St. James. And once a bottle of Cte Rtie or Scharlachberger is in her, even the least emotional woman shows the same complex of sentimentalities that a man shows, and is as maudlin and idiotic as he is.

Nay; the superior acumen and self-possession of women is not inherent in any peculiarity of their constitutions, and above all, not in any advantage of a purely physical character. Its springs are rather to be sought in a physical disadvantage—that is, in the mechanical inferiority of their frames, their relative lack of tractive capacity, their deficiency as brute engines. That deficiency, as every one knows, is partly a derricked heritage from those females of the Pongo pygmaeus who were their probable fore-runners in the world; the same thing is to be observed in the females of almost all other species of mammals. But it is also partly due to the effects of use under civilization, and, above all, to what evolutionists call sexual selection. In other words, women were already measurably weaker than men at the dawn of human history, and that relative weakness has been progressively augmented in the interval by the conditions of human life. For one thing, the process of bringing forth young has become so much more exhausting as refinement has replaced savage sturdiness and callousness, and the care of them in infancy has become so much more onerous as the growth of cultural complexity has made education more intricate, that the two functions now lay vastly heavier burdens upon the strength and attention of a woman than they lay upon the strength and attention of any other female. And for another thing, the consequent disability and need of physical protection, by feeding and inflaming the already large vanity of man, have caused him to attach a concept of attractiveness to feminine weakness, so that he has come to esteem his woman, not in proportion as she is self-sufficient as a social animal but in proportion as she is dependent. In this vicious circle of influences women have been caught, and as a result their chief physical character today is their fragility. A woman cannot lift as much as a man. She cannot walk as far. She cannot exert as much mechanical energy in any other way. Even her alleged superior endurance, as Havelock Ellis has demonstrated in "Man and Woman," is almost wholly mythical; she cannot, in point of fact, stand nearly so much hardship as aman can stand, and so the law, usually an ass, exhibits an unaccustomed accuracy of observation in its assumption that, whenever husband and wife are exposed alike to fatal suffering, say in a shipwreck, the wife dies first.

So far we have been among platitudes. There is less of overt platitude in the doctrine that it is precisely this physical frailty that has given women their peculiar nimbleness and effectiveness on the intellectual side. Nevertheless, it is equally true. What they have done is what every healthy and elastic organism does in like case; they have sought compensation for their impotence in one field by employing their resources in another field to the utmost, and out of that constant and maximum use has come a marked enlargement of those resources. On the one hand the sum of them present in a given woman has been enormously increased by natural selection, so that every woman, so to speak, inherits a certain extra-masculine mental dexterity as a mere function of her femaleness. And on the other hand every woman, over and above this almost unescapable legacy from her actual grandmothers, also inherits admission to that traditional wisdom which constitutes the esoteric philosophy of woman as a whole. The virgin at adolescence is thus in the position of an unusually fortunate apprentice, for she is not only naturally gifted but also apprenticed to extraordinarily competent masters. While a boy at the same period is learning from his elders little more than a few empty technical tricks, a few paltry vices and a few degrading enthusiasms, his sister is under instruction in all those higher exercises of the wits that her special deficiencies make necessary to her security, and in particular in all those exercises which aim at overcoming the physical, and hence social and economic superiority of man by attacks upon his inferior capacity for clear reasoning, uncorrupted by illusion and sentimentality.

12.

Honour

Here, it is obvious, the process of intellectual development takes colour from the Sklavenmoral, and is, in a sense, a product of it. The Jews, as Nietzsche has demonstrated, got their unusual intelligence by the same process; a contrary process is working in the case of the English and the Americans, and has begun to show itself in the case of the French and Germans. The sum of feminine wisdom that I have just mentioned—the body of feminine devices and competences that is handed down from generation to generation of women—is, in fact, made up very largely of doctrines and expedients that infallibly appear to the average sentimental man, helpless as he is before them, as cynical and immoral. He commonly puts this aversion into the theory that women have no sense of honour. The criticism, of course, is characteristically banal. Honour is a concept too tangled to be analyzed here, but it may be sufficient to point out that it is predicated upon a feeling of absolute security, and that, in that capital conflict between man and woman out of which rises most of man's complaint of its absence—to wit, the conflict culminating in marriage, already described—the security of the woman is not something that is in actual being, but something that she is striving with all arms to attain. In such a conflict it must be manifest that honor can have no place. An animal fighting for its very existence uses all possible means of offence and defence, however foul. Even man, for all his boasting about honor, seldom displays it when he has anything of the first value at hazard. He is honorable, perhaps, in gambling, for gambling is a mere vice, but it is quite unusual for him to be honorable in business, for business is bread and butter. He is honorable (so long as the stake is trivial) in his sports, but he seldom permits honor to interfere with his perjuries in a lawsuit, or with hitting below the belt in any other sort of combat that is in earnest. The history of all his wars is a history of mutual allegations of dishonorable practices, and such allegations are nearly always well grounded. The best imitation of honor that he ever actually achieves in them is a highly self-conscious sentimentality which prompts him to be humane to the opponent who has been wounded, or disarmed, or otherwise made innocuous. Even here his so-called honor is little more than a form of playacting, both maudlin and dishonest. In the actual death-struggle he invariably bites.

Perhaps one of the chief charms of woman lies precisely in the fact that they are dishonorable, i.e., that they are relatively uncivilized. In the midst of all the puerile repressions and inhibitions that hedge them round, they continue to show a gipsy spirit. No genuine woman ever gives a hoot for law if law happens to stand in the way of her private interest. She is essentially an outlaw, a rebel, what H. G. Wells calls a nomad. The boons of civilization are so noisily cried up by sentimentalists that we are all apt to overlook its disadvantages. Intrinsically, it is a mere device for regimenting men. Its perfect symbol is the goose-step. The most civilized man is simply that man who has been most successful in caging and harnessing his honest and natural instincts-that is, the man who has done most cruel violence to his own ego in the interest of the commonweal. The value of this commonweal is always overestimated. What is it at bottom? Simply the greatest good to the greatest number—of petty rogues, ignoramuses and poltroons.

The capacity for submitting to and prospering comfortably under this cheese-monger's civilization is far more marked in men than in women, and far more in inferior men than in men of the higher categories. It must be obvious to even so pathetic an ass as a university professor of history that very few of the genuinely first-rate men of the race have been, wholly civilized, in the sense that the term is employed in newspapers and in the pulpit. Think of Caesar, Bonaparte, Luther, Frederick the Great, Cromwell, Barbarossa, Innocent III, Bolivar, Hannibal, Alexander, and to come down to our own time, Grant, Stonewall Jackson, Bismarck, Wagner, Garibaldi and Cecil Rhodes.

13.

Women and the Emotions

The fact that women have a greater capacity than men for controlling and concealing their emotions is not an indication that they are more civilized, but a proof that they are less civilized. This capacity, so rare today, and withal so valuable and worthy of respect, is a characteristic of savages, not of civilized men, and its loss is one of the penalties that the race has paid for the tawdry boon of civilization. Your true savage, reserved, dignified, and courteous, knows how to mask his feelings, even in the face of the most desperate assault upon them; your civilized man is forever yielding to them. Civilization, in fact, grows more and more maudlin and hysterical; especially under democracy it tends to degenerate into a mere combat of crazes; the whole aim of practical politics is to keep the populace alarmed (and hence clamorous to be led to safety) by an endless series of hobgoblins, most of them imaginary. Wars are no longer waged by the will of superior men, capable of judging dispassionately and intelligently the causes behind them and the effects flowing out of them. They are now begun by first throwing a mob into a panic; they are ended only when it has spent its ferine fury. Here the effect of civilization has been to reduce the noblest of the arts, once the repository of an exalted etiquette and the chosen avocation of the very best men of the race, to the level of a riot of peasants. All the wars of Christendom are now disgusting and degrading; the conduct of them has passed out of the hands of nobles and knights and into the, hands of mob-orators, money-lenders, and atrocity-mongers. To recreate one's self with war in the grand manner, as Prince Eugene, Marlborough and the Old Dessauer knew it, one must now go among barbarian peoples.

Women are nearly always against war in modern times, for the reasons brought forward to justify it are usually either transparently dishonest or childishly sentimental, and hence provoke their scorn. But once the business is begun, they commonly favour its conduct outrance, and are thus in accord with the theory of the great captains of more spacious days. In Germany, during the late war, the protests against the Schrecklichkeit practised by the imperial army and navy did not come from women, but from sentimental men; in England and the United States there is no record that any woman ever raised her voice against the blockade which destroyed hundreds of thousands of German children. I was on both sides of the bloody chasm during the war, and I cannot recall meeting a single woman who subscribed to the puerile doctrine that, in so vast a combat between nations, there could still be categories of non-combatants, with aright of asylum on armed ships and in garrisoned towns. This imbecility was maintained only by men, large numbers of whom simultaneously took part in wholesale massacres of such non-combatants. The women were superior to such hypocrisy. They recognized the nature of modern war instantly and accurately, and advocated no disingenuous efforts to conceal it.

14.

Pseudo-Anaesthesia

The feminine talent for concealing emotion is probably largely responsible for the common masculine belief that women are devoid of passion, and contemplate its manifestations in the male with something akin to trembling. Here the talent itself is helped out by the fact that very few masculine observers, on the occasions when they give attention to the matter, are in a state of mind conducive to exact observation. The truth is, of course, that there is absolutely no reason to believe that the normal woman is passionless, or that the minority of women who unquestionably are is of formidable dimensions. To be sure, the peculiar vanity of men, particularly in the Northern countries, makes them place a high value upon the virginal type of woman, and so this type tends to grow more common by sexual selection, but despite that fact, it has by no means superseded the normal type, so realistically described by the theologians and publicists of the Middle Ages. It would, however, be rash to assert that this long continued sexual selection has not made itself felt, even in the normal type. Its chief effect, perhaps, is to make it measurably easier for a woman to conquer and conceal emotion than it is for a man. But this is a mere reinforcement of a native quality or, at all events, a quality long antedating the rise of the curious preference just mentioned. That preference obviously owes its origin to the concept of private property and is most evident in those countries in which the largest proportion of males are property owners, i.e.,in which the property-owning caste reaches down into the lowest conceivable strata of bounders and ignoramuses. The low-caste man is never quite sure of his wife unless he is convinced that she is entirely devoid of amorous susceptibility. Thus he grows uneasy whenever she shows any sign of responding in kind to his own elephantine emotions, and is apt to be suspicious of even so trivial a thing as a hearty response to a connubial kiss. If he could manage to rid himself of such suspicions, there would be less public gabble about anesthetic wives, and fewer books written by quacks with sure cures for them, and a good deal less cold-mutton formalism and boredom at the domestic hearth.

I have a feeling that the husband of this sort—he is very common in the United States, and almost as common among the middle classes of England, Germany and Scandinavia—does himself a serious disservice, and that he is uneasily conscious of it. Having got himself a wife to his austere taste, he finds that she is rather depressing—that his vanity is almost as painfully damaged by her emotional inertness as it would have been by a too provocative and hedonistic spirit. For the thing that chiefly delights a man, when some, woman has gone through the solemn buffoonery of yielding to his great love, is the sharp and flattering contrast between her reserve in the presence of other men and her enchanting complaisance in the presence of himself. Here his vanity is enormously tickled. To the world in general she seems remote and unapproachable; to him she is docile, fluttering, gurgling, even a bit abandoned. It is as if some great magnifico male, some inordinate czar or kaiser, should step down from the throne to play dominoes with him behind the door. The greater the contrast between the lady's two fronts, the greater his satisfaction-up to, of course, the point where his suspicions are aroused. Let her diminish that contrast ever so little on the public side—by smiling at a handsome actor, by saying a word too many to an attentive head-waiter, by holding the hand of the rector of the parish, by winking amiably at his brother or at her sister'husband—and at once the poor fellow begins to look for clandestine notes, to employ private inquiry agents, and to scrutinize the eyes, ears, noses and hair of his children with shameful doubts. This explains many domestic catastrophes.

15.

Mythical Anthropophagi

The man-hating woman, like the cold woman, is largely imaginary. One often encounters references to her in literature, but who has ever met hex in real life? As for me, I doubt that such a monster has ever actually existed. There are, of course, women who spend a great deal of time denouncing and reviling men, but these are certainly not genuine man-haters; they are simply women who have done their utmost to snare men, and failed. Of such sort are the majority of inflammatory suffragettes of the sex-hygiene and birth-control species. The rigid limitation of offspring, in fact, is chiefly advocated by women who run no more risk of having unwilling motherhood forced upon them than so many mummies of the Tenth Dynasty. All their unhealthy interest in such noisome matters has behind it merely a subconscious yearning to attract the attention of men, who are supposed to be partial to enterprises that are difficult or forbidden. But certainly the enterprise of dissuading such a propagandist from her gospel would not be difficult, and I know of no law forbidding it.

I'll begin to believe in the man-hater the day I am introduced to a woman who has definitely and finally refused a chance of marriage to aman who is of her own station in life, able to support her, unafflicted by any loathsome disease, and of reasonably decent aspect and manners—in brief a man who is thoroughly eligible. I doubt that any such woman breathes the air of Christendom. Whenever one comes to confidential terms with an unmarried woman, of course, she favours one with a long chronicle of the men she has refused to marry, greatly to their grief. But unsentimental cross-examination, at least in my experience, always develops the fact that every one of these suffered from some obvious and intolerable disqualification. Either he had a wife already and was vague about his ability to get rid of her, or he was drunk when he was brought to his proposal and repudiated it or forgot it the next day, or he was a bankrupt, or he was old and decrepit, or he was young and plainly idiotic, or he had diabetes or a bad heart, or his relatives were impossible, or he believed in spiritualism, or democracy, or the Baconian theory, or some other such nonsense. Restricting the thing to men palpably eligible, I believe thoroughly that no sane woman has ever actually muffed a chance. Now and then, perhaps, a miraculously fortunate girl has two victims on the mat simultaneously, and has to lose one. But they are seldom, if ever, both good chances; one is nearly always a duffer, thrown in in the telling to make the bourgeoisie marvel.

16.

A Conspiracy of Silence

The reason why all this has to be stated here is simply that women, who could state it much better, have almost unanimously refrained from discussing such matters at all. One finds, indeed, a sort of general conspiracy, infinitely alert and jealous, against the publication of the esoteric wisdom of the sex, and even against the acknowledgment that any such body of erudition exists at all. Men, having more vanity and less discretion, area good deal less cautious. There is, in fact, a whole literature of masculine babbling, ranging from Machiavelli's appalling confession of political theory to the egoistic confidences of such men as Nietzsche, Jean-Jacques Rousseau, Casanova, Max Stirner, Benvenuto Cellini, Napoleon Bonaparte and Lord Chesterfield. But it is very rarely that a Marie Bashkirtsev or Margot Asquith lets down the veils which conceal the acroamatic doctrine of the other sex. It is transmitted from mother to daughter, so to speak, behind the door. One observes its practical workings, but hears little about its principles. The causes of this secrecy are obvious. Women, in the last analysis, can prevail against men in the great struggle for power and security only by keeping them disarmed, and, in the main, unwarned. In a pitched battle, with the devil taking the hindmost, their physical and economic inferiority would inevitably bring them to disaster. Thus they have to apply their peculiar talents warily, and with due regard to the danger of arousing the foe. He must be attached without any formal challenge, and even without any suspicion of challenge. This strategy lies at the heart of what Nietzsche called the slave morality—in brief, a morality based upon a concealment of egoistic purpose, a code of ethics having for its foremost character a bold denial of its actual aim.

III

Marriage

17.

Fundamental Motives

How successful such a concealment may be is well displayed by the general acceptance of the notion that women are reluctant to enter into marriage—that they have to be persuaded to it by eloquence and pertinacity, and even by a sort of intimidation. The truth is that, in a world almost divested of intelligible idealism, and hence dominated by a senseless worship of the practical, marriage offers the best career that the average woman can reasonably aspire to, and, in the case of very many women, the only one that actually offers a livelihood. What is esteemed and valuable, in our materialistic and unintelligent society, is precisely that petty practical efficiency at which men are expert, and which serves them in place of free intelligence. A woman, save she show a masculine strain that verges upon the pathological, cannot hope to challenge men in general in this department, but it is always open to her to exchange her sexual charm for a lion's share in the earnings of one man, and this is what she almost invariably tries to do. That is to say, she tries to get a husband, for getting a husband means, in a sense, enslaving an expert, and so covering up her own lack of expertness, and escaping its consequences. Thereafter she has at least one stout line of defence against a struggle for existence in which the prospect of survival is chiefly based, not upon the talents that are typically hers, but upon those that she typically lacks. Before the average woman succumbs in this struggle, some man or other must succumb first. Thus her craft converts her handicap into an advantage.

In this security lies the most important of all the benefits that a woman attains by marriage. It is, in fact, the most important benefit that the mind can imagine, for the whole effort of the human race, under our industrial society, is concentrated upon the attainment of it. But there are other benefits, too. One of them is that increase in dignity which goes with an obvious success; the woman who has got herself a satisfactory husband, or even a highly imperfect husband, is regarded with respect by other women, and has a contemptuous patronage for those who have failed to do likewise. Again, marriage offers her the only safe opportunity, considering the levantine view of women as property which Christianity has preserved in our civilization, to obtain gratification for that powerful complex of instincts which we call the sexual, and, in particular, for the instinct of maternity. The woman who has not had a child remains incomplete, ill at ease, and more than a little ridiculous. She is in the position of a man who has never stood in battle; she has missed the most colossal experience of her sex. Moreover, a social odium goes with her loss. Other women regard her as a sort of permanent tyro, and treat her with ill-concealed disdain, and deride the very virtue which lies at the bottom of her experiential penury. There would seem to be, indeed, but small respect among women for virginity per se. They are against the woman who has got rid of hers outside marriage, not because they think she has lost anything intrinsically valuable, but because she has made a bad bargain, and one that materially diminishes the sentimental respect for virtue held by men, and hence one against the general advantage an dwell-being of the sex. In other words, it is a guild resentment that they feel, not a moral resentment. Women, in general, are not actively moral, nor, for that matter, noticeably modest. Every man, indeed, who is in wide practice among them is occasionally astounded and horrified to discover, on some rainy afternoon, an almost complete absence of modesty in some women of the highest respectability.

But of all things that a woman gains by marriage the most valuable is economic security. Such security, of course, is seldom absolute, but usually merely relative: the best provider among husbands may die without enough life insurance, or run off with some preposterous light of love, or become an invalid or insane, or step over the intangible and wavering line which separates business success from a prison cell. Again, a woman may be deceived: there are stray women who are credulous and sentimental, and stray men who are cunning. Yet again, a woman may make false deductions from evidence accurately before her, ineptly guessing that the clerk she marries today will be the head of the firm tomorrow, instead of merely the bookkeeper tomorrow. But on the whole it must be plain that a woman, in marrying, usually obtains for herself a reasonably secure position in that station of life to which she is accustomed. She seeks a husband, not sentimentally, but realistically; she always gives thought to the economic situation; she seldom takes a chance if it is possible to avoid it. It is common for men to marry women who bring nothing to the joint capital of marriage save good looks and an appearance of vivacity; it is almost unheard of for women to neglect more prosaic inquiries. Many a rich man, at least in America, marries his typist or the governess of his sister's children and is happy thereafter, but when a rare woman enters upon a comparable marriage she is commonly set down as insane, and the disaster that almost always ensues quickly confirms the diagnosis.

The economic and social advantage that women thus seek in marriage—and the seeking is visible no less in the kitchen wench who aspires to the heart of a policeman than in the fashionable flapper who looks for a husband with a Rolls-Royce—is, by a curious twist of fate, one of the underlying causes of their precarious economic condition before marriage rescues them. In a civilization which lays its greatest stress upon an uninspired and almost automatic expertness, and offers its highest rewards to the more intricate forms thereof, they suffer the disadvantage of being less capable of it than men. Part of this disadvantage, as we have seen, is congenital; their very intellectual enterprise makes it difficult for them to become the efficient machines that men are. But part of it is also due to the fact that, with marriage always before them, coloring their every vision of the future, and holding out a steady promise of swift and complete relief, they are under no such implacable pressure as men are to acquire the sordid arts they revolt against. The time is too short and the incentive too feeble. Before the woman employs of twenty-one can master a tenth of the idiotic "knowledge" in the head of the male clerk of thirty, or even convince herself that it is worth mastering, she has married the head of the establishment or maybe the clerk himself, and so abandons the business. It is, indeed, not until a woman has definitely put away the hope of marriage, or, at all events, admitted the possibility that she, may have to do so soon or late, that she buckles down in earnest to whatever craft she practises, and makes a genuine effort to develop competence. No sane man, seeking a woman for a post requiring laborious training and unremitting diligence, would select a woman still definitely young and marriageable. To the contrary, he would choose either a woman so unattractive sexually as to be palpably incapable of snaring a man, or one so embittered by some catastrophe of amour as to be pathologically emptied of the normal aspirations of her sex.

18.

The Process of Courtship

This bemusement of the typical woman by the notion of marriage has been noted as self-evident by every literate student of the phenomena of sex, from the early Christian fathers down to Nietzsche, Ellis and Shaw. That It is denied by the current sentimentality of Christendom is surely no evidence against it. What we have in this denial, as I have said, is no more than a proof of woman's talent for a high and sardonic form of comedy and of man's infinite vanity. "I wooed and won her," says Sganarelle of his wife. "I made him run," says the hare of the hound. When the thing is maintained, not as a mere windy sentimentality, but with some notion of carrying it logically, the result is invariably a display of paralogy so absurd that it becomes pathetic. Such nonsense one looks for in the works of gyneophile theorists with no experience of the world, and there is where one finds it. It is almost always wedded to the astounding doctrine that sexual frigidity, already disposed of, is normal in the female, and that the approach of the male is made possible, not by its melting into passion, but by a purely intellectual determination, inwardly revolting, to avoid his ire by pandering to his gross appetites. Thus the thing is stated in a book called "The Sexes in Science and History," by Eliza Burt Gamble, an American lady anthropologist:

The beautiful coloring of male birds and fishes, and the various appendages acquired by males throughout the various orders below man, and which, sofar as they themselves are concerned, serve no other useful purpose than to aid them in securing the favours of the females, have by the latter been turned to account in the processes of reproduction. The female made the male beautiful THAT SHE MIGHT ENDURE HIS CARESSES.

The italics are mine. From this premiss the learned doctor proceeds to the classical sentimental argument that the males of all species, including man, are little more than chronic seducers, and that their chief energies are devoted to assaulting and breaking down the native reluctance of the aesthetic and anesthetic females. In her own words: "Regarding males, outside of the instinct for self-preservation, which, by the way is often overshadowed by their great sexual eagerness, no discriminating characters have been acquired and transmitted, other than those which have been the result of passion, namely, pugnacity and perseverance." Again the italics are mine. What we have here is merely the old, old delusion of masculine enterprise in amour—the concept of man as a lascivious monster and of woman as his shrinking victim—in brief, the Don Juan idea in fresh bib and tucker. In such bilge lie the springs of many of the most vexatious delusions of the world, and of some of its loudest farce no less. It is thus that fatuous old maids are led to look under their beds for fabulous ravishers, and to cry out that they have been stabbed with hypodermic needles in cinema theatres, and to watch furtively for white slavers in railroad stations. It is thus, indeed, that the whole white-slave mountebankery has been launched, with its gaudy fictions and preposterous alarms. And it is thus, more importantly, that whole regiments of neurotic wives have been convinced that their children are monuments, not to a co-operation in which their own share was innocent and cordial, but to the solitary libidinousness of their swinish and unconscionable husbands.

Dr. Gamble, of course, is speaking of the lower fauna in the time of Noah. A literal application of her theory toman today is enough to bring it to a reductio ad absurdum. Which sex of Homo sapiens actually does the primping and parading that she describes? Which runs to "beautiful coloring," sartorial, hirsute, facial? Which encases itself in vestments which "serve no other useful purpose than to aid in securing the favours" of the other? The insecurity of the gifted savante's` position is at once apparent. The more convincingly she argues that the primeval mud-hens and she mackerel had to be anesthetized with spectacular decorations in order to "endure the caresses" of their beaux, the more she supports the thesis that men have to be decoyed and bamboozled into love today. In other words, her argument turns upon and destroys itself. Carried to its last implication, it holds that women are all Donna Juanitas, and that if they put off their millinery and cosmetics, and abandoned the shameless sexual allurements of their scanty dress, men could not "endure their caresses."

To be sure, Dr. Gamble by no means draws this disconcerting conclusion herself. To the contrary, she clings to the conventional theory that the human female of today is no more than the plaything of the concupiscent male, and that she must wait for the feminist millenium to set her free from his abominable pawings. But she can reach this notion only by standing her whole structure of reasoning on its head—in fact, by knocking it over and repudiating it. On the one hand, she argues that splendour of attire is merely a bait to overcome the reluctance of the opposite sex, and on the other hand she argues, at least by fair inference, that it is not. This grotesque switching of horses, however, need not detain us. The facts are too plain to be disposed of by a lady anthropologist's theorizings. Those facts are supported, in the field of animal behaviour, by the almost unanimous evidence of zoologists, including that of Dr. Gamble herself. They are supported, in the field of human behaviour, by a body of observation and experience so colossal that it would be quite out of the question to dispose of it. Women, as I have shown, have a more delicate aesthetic sense than men; in a world wholly rid of men they would probably still array themselves with vastly more care and thought of beauty than men would ever show in like case. But with the world what it is, it must be obvious that their display of finery—to say nothing of their display of epidermis—has the conscious purpose of attracting the masculine eye. Anormal woman, indeed, never so much as buys a pair of shoes or has her teeth plugged without considering, in the back of her mind, the effect upon some unsuspecting candidate for her "reluctant" affections.

19.

The Actual Husband

So far as I can make out, no woman of the sort worth hearing—that is, no woman of intelligence, humour and charm, and hence of success in the duel of sex—has ever publicly denied this; the denial is confined entirely to the absurd sect of female bachelors of arts and to the generality of vain and unobservant men. The former, having failed to attract men by the devices described, take refuge behind the sour grapes doctrine that they have never tried, and the latter, having fallen victims, sooth their egoism by arrogating the whole agency to themselves, thus giving it a specious appearance of the volitional, and even of the, audacious. The average man is an almost incredible popinjay; he can think of himself only as at the centre of situations. All the, sordid transactions of his life appear to him, and are depicted in his accounts of them, as feats, successes, proofs of his acumen. He regards it as an almost magical exploit to operate a stock-brokerage shop, or to get elected to public office, or to swindle his fellow knaves in some degrading commercial enterprise, or to profess some nonsense or other in a college, or to write so platitudinous a book as this one. And in the same way he views it as a great testimony to his prowess at amour to yield up his liberty, his property and his soul to the first woman who, in despair of finding better game, turns her appraising eye upon him. But if you want to hear a mirthless laugh, just present this masculine theory to a bridesmaid at a wedding, particularly after alcohol and crocodile tears have done their disarming work upon her. That is to say, just hint to her that the bride harboured no notion of marriage until stormed into acquiescence by the moonstruck and impetuous bridegroom.

I have used the phrase, "in despair of finding better game." What I mean is this that not one woman in a hundred ever marries her first choice among marriageable men. That first choice is almost invariably one who is beyond her talents, for reasons either fortuitous or intrinsic. Let us take, for example, a woman whose relative navetete makes the process clearly apparent, to wit, a simple shop-girl. Her absolute first choice, perhaps, is not a living man at all, but a supernatural abstraction in a book, say, one of the heroes of Hall Caine, Ethel M.Dell, or Marie Corelli. After him comes a moving-picture actor. Then another moving-picture actor. Then, perhaps, many more—ten or fifteen head. Then a sebaceous young clergyman. Then the junior partner in the firm she works for. Then a couple of department managers. Then a clerk. Then a young man with no definite profession or permanent job—one of the innumerable host which flits from post to post, always restive, always trying something new—perhaps a neighborhood garage-keeper in the end. Well, the girl begins with the Caine colossus: he vanishes into thin air. She proceeds to the moving picture actors: they are almost as far beyond her. And then to the man of God, the junior partner, the department manager, the clerk; one and all they are carried off by girls of greater attractions and greater skill—girls who can cast gaudier flies. In the end, suddenly terrorized by the first faint shadows of spinsterhood, she turns to the ultimate numskull—and marries him out of hand.

This, allowing for class modifications, is almost the normal history of a marriage, or, more accurately, of the genesis of a marriage, under Protestant Christianity. Under other rites the business is taken out of the woman's hands, at least partly, and so she is less enterprising in her assembling of candidates and possibilities. But when the whole thing is left to her own heart—i.e., to her head—it is but natural that she should seek as wide a range of choice as the conditions of her life allow, and in a democratic society those conditions put few if any fetters upon her fancy. The servant girl, or factory operative, or even prostitute of today may be the chorus girl or moving picture vampire of tomorrow and the millionaire's wife of next year. In America, especially, men have no settled antipathy to such stooping alliances; in fact, it rather flatters their vanity to play Prince Charming to Cinderella. The result is that every normal American young woman, with the practicality of her sex and the inner confidence that goes therewith, raises her amorous eye as high as it will roll. And the second result is that every American man of presentable exterior and easy means is surrounded by an aura of discreet provocation: he cannot even dictate a letter, or ask for a telephone number without being measured for his wedding coat. On the Continent of Europe, and especially in the Latin countries, where class barriers are more formidable, the situation differs materially, and to the disadvantage of the girl. If she makes an overture, it is an invitation to disaster; her hope of lawful marriage by such means is almost nil. In consequence, the prudent and decent girl avoids such overtures, and they must be made by third parties or by the man himself. This is the explanation of the fact that a Frenchman, say, is habitually enterprising in amour, and hence bold and often offensive, whereas an American is what is called chivalrous. The American is chivalrous for the simple reason that the initiative is not in his hands. His chivalry is really a sort of coquetry.

20.

The Unattainable Ideal

But here I rather depart from the point, which is this: that the average woman is not strategically capable of bringing down the most tempting game within her purview, and must thus content herself with a second, third, or nth choice. The only women who get their first choices are those who run in almost miraculous luck and those too stupid to formulate an ideal—two very small classes, it must be obvious. A few women, true enough, are so pertinacious that they prefer defeat to compromise. That is to say, they prefer to put off marriage indefinitely rather than to marry beneath the highest leap of their fancy. But such women may be quickly dismissed as abnormal, and perhaps as downright diseased in mind; the average woman is well-aware that marriage is far better for her than celibacy, even when it falls a good deal short of her primary hopes, and she is also well aware that the differences between man and man, once mere money is put aside, are so slight as to be practically almost negligible. Thus the average woman is under none of the common masculine illusions about elective affinities, soul mates, love at first sight, and such phantasms. She is quite ready to fall in love, as the phrase is, with any man who is plainly eligible, and she usually knows a good many more such men than one. Her primary demand in marriage is not for the agonies of romance, but for comfort and security; she is thus easier satisfied than a man, and oftener happy. One frequently hears of remarried widowers who continue to moon about their dead first wives, but for a remarried widow to show any such sentimentality would be a nine days' wonder. Once replaced, a dead husband is expunged from the minutes. And so is a dead love.

One of the results of all this is a subtle reinforcement of the contempt with which women normally regard their husbands—a contempt grounded, as I have shown, upon a sense of intellectual superiority. To this primary sense of superiority is now added the disparagement of a concrete comparison, and over all is an ineradicable resentment of the fact that such a comparison has been necessary. In other words, the typical husband is a second-rater, and no one is better aware of it than his wife. He is, taking averages, one who has been loved, as the saying goes, by but one woman, and then only as a second, third or nth choice. If any other woman had ever loved him, as the idiom has it, she would have married him, and so made him ineligible for his present happiness. But the average bachelor is a man who has been loved, so to speak, by many women, and is the lost first choice of at least some of them. Here presents the unattainable, and hence the admirable; the husband is the attained and disdained.

Here we have a sufficient explanation of the general superiority of bachelors, so often noted by students of mankind—a superiority so marked that it is difficult, in all history, to find six first-rate philosophers who were married men. The bachelor's very capacity to avoid marriage is no more than a proof of his relative freedom from the ordinary sentimentalism of his sex—in other words, of his greater approximation to the clear headedness of the enemy sex. He is able to defeat the enterprise of women because he brings to the business an equipment almost comparable to their own. Herbert Spencer, until he was fifty, was ferociously harassed by women of all sorts. Among others, George Eliot tried very desperately to marry him. But after he had made it plain, over a long series of years, that he was prepared to resist marriage to the full extent of his military and naval power, the girls dropped off one by one, and so his last decades were full of peace and he got a great deal of very important work done.

21.

The Effect on the Race

It is, of course, not well for the world that the highest sort of men are thus selected out, as the biologists say, and that their superiority dies with them, whereas the ignoble tricks and sentimentalities of lesser men are infinitely propagated. Despite a popular delusion that the sons of great men are always dolts, the fact is that intellectual superiority is inheritable, quite as easily as bodily strength; and that fact has been established beyond cavil by the laborious inquiries of Galton, Pearson and the other anthropometricians of the English school. If such men as Spinoza, Kant, Schopenhauer, Spencer, and Nietzsche had married and begotten sons, those sons, it is probable, would have contributed as much to philosophy as the sons and grandsons of Veit Bach contributed to music, or those of Erasmus Darwin to biology, or those of Henry Adams to politics, or those of Hamilcar Barcato the art of war. I have said that Herbert Spencer's escape from marriage facilitated his life-work, and so served the immediate good of English philosophy, but in the long run it will work a detriment, for he left no sons to carry on his labours, and the remaining Englishmen of his time were unable to supply the lack. His celibacy, indeed, made English philosophy co-extensive with his life; since his death the whole body of metaphysical speculation produced in England has been of little more, practical value to the world than a drove of bogs. In precisely the same way the celibacy of Schopenhauer, Kant and Nietzsche has reduced German philosophy to feebleness.

Even setting aside this direct influence of heredity, there is the equally potent influence of example and tuition. It is a gigantic advantage to live on intimate terms with a first-rate, man, and have his care. Hamilcar not only gave the Carthagenians a great general in his actual son; he also gave them a great general in his son-in-law, trained in his camp. But the tendency of the first-rate man to remain a bachelor is very strong, and Sidney Lee once showed that, of all the great writers of England since the Renaissance, more than half were either celibates or lived apart from their wives. Even the married ones revealed the tendency plainly. For example, consider Shakespeare. He was forced into marriage while still a minor by the brothers of Ann Hathaway, who was several years his senior, and had debauched him and gave out that she was enceinte by him. He escaped from her abhorrent embraces as quickly as possible, and thereafter kept as far away from her as he could. His very distaste for marriage, indeed, was the cause of his residence in London, and hence, in all probability, of the labours which made him immortal.

In different parts of the world various expedients have been resorted to to overcome this reluctance to marriage among the, better sort of men. Christianity, in general, combats it on the ground that it is offensive to God—though at the same, time leaning toward an enforced celibacy among its own agents. The discrepancy is fatal to the position. On the one hand, it is impossible to believe that the same God who permitted His own son to die a bachelor regards celibacy as an actual sin, and on the other hand, it is obvious that the average cleric would be damaged but little, and probably improved appreciably, by having a wife to think for him, and to force him to virtue and industry, and to aid him otherwise in his sordid profession. Where religious superstitions have died out the institution of the dot prevails—an idea borrowed by Christians from the Jews. The dot is simply a bribe designed to overcome the disinclination of the male. It involves a frank recognition of the fact that he loses by marriage, and it seeks to make up for that loss by a money payment. Its obvious effect is to give young women a wider and better choice of husbands. A relatively superior man, otherwise quite out of reach, may be brought into camp by the assurance of economic ease, and what is more, he may be kept in order after he has been taken by the consciousness of his gain. Among hardheaded and highly practical peoples, such as the Jews and the French, the dot flourishes, and its effect is to promote intellectual suppleness in the race, for the average child is thus not inevitably the offspring of a woman and a noodle, as with us, but may be the offspring of a woman and a man of reasonable intelligence. But even in France, the very highest class of men tend to evade marriage; they resist money almost as unanimously as their Anglo-Saxon brethren resist sentimentality.

In America the dot is almost unknown, partly because money-getting is easier to men than in Europe and is regarded as less degrading, and partly because American men are more naive than Frenchmen and are thus readily intrigued without actual bribery. But the best of them nevertheless lean to celibacy, and plans for overcoming their habit are frequently proposed and discussed. One such plan involves a heavy tax on bachelors. The defect in it lies in the fact that the average bachelor, for obvious reasons, is relatively well to do, and would pay the tax rather than marry. Moreover, the payment of it would help to salve his conscience, which is now often made restive, I believe, by a maudlin feeling that he is shirking his duty to the race, and so he would be confirmed and supported in his determination to avoid the altar. Still further, he would escape the social odium which now attaches to his celibacy, for whatever a man pays for is regarded as his right. As things stand, that odium is of definite potency, and undoubtedly has its influence upon a certain number of men in the lower ranks of bachelors. They stand, so to speak, in the twilight zone of bachelorhood, with one leg furtively over the altar rail; it needs only an extra pull to bring them to the sacrifice. But if they could compound for their immunity by a cash indemnity it is highly probable that they would take on new resolution, and in the end they would convert what remained of their present disrepute into a source of egoistic satisfaction, as is done, indeed, by a great many bachelors even today. These last immoralists are privy to the elements which enter into that disrepute: the ire of women whose devices they have resisted and the envy of men who have succumbed.

22.

Compulsory Marriage

I myself once proposed an alternative scheme, to wit, the prohibition of sentimental marriages by law, and the substitution of match-making by the common hangman. This plan, as revolutionary as it may seem, would have several plain advantages. For one thing, it would purge the serious business of marriage of the romantic fol-de-rol that now corrupts it, and so make for the peace and happiness of the race. For another thing, it would work against the process which now selects out, as I have said, those men who are most fit, and so throws the chief burden of paternity upon the inferior, to the damage of posterity. The hangman, if he made his selections arbitrarily, would try to give his office permanence and dignity by choosing men whose marriage would meet with public approbation, i.e., men obviously of sound stock and talents, i.e., the sort of men who now habitually escape. And if he made his selection by the hazard of the die, or by drawing numbers out of a hat, or by any other such method of pure chance, that pure chance would fall indiscriminately upon all orders of men, and the upper orders would thus lose their present comparative immunity. True enough, a good many men would endeavour to influence him privately to their own advantage, and it is probable that he would occasionally succumb, but it must be plain that the men most likely to prevail in that enterprise would not be philosophers, but politicians, and so there would be some benefit to the race even here. Posterity surely suffers no very heavy loss when a Congressman, a member of the House of Lords or even an ambassador or Prime Minister dies childless, but when a Herbert Spencer goes to the grave without leaving sons behind him there is a detriment to all the generations of the future.

I did not offer the plan, of course, as a contribution to practical politics, but merely as a sort of hypothesis, to help clarify the problem. Many other theoretical advantages appear in it, but its execution is made impossible, not only by inherent defects, but also by a general disinclination to abandon the present system, which at least offers certain attractions to concrete men and women, despite its unfavourable effects upon the unborn. Women would oppose the substitution of chance or arbitrary fiat for the existing struggle for the plain reason that every woman is convinced, and no doubt rightly, that her own judgment is superior to that of either the common hangman or the gods, and that her own enterprise is more favourable to her opportunities. And men would oppose it because it would restrict their liberty. This liberty, of course, is largely imaginary. In its common manifestation, it is no more, at bottom, than the privilege of being bamboozled and made a mock of by the, first woman who ventures to essay the business. But none the less it is quite as precious to menas any other of the ghosts that their vanity conjures up for their enchantment. They cherish the notion that unconditioned volition enters into the matter, and that under volition there is not only a high degree of sagacity but also a touch of the daring and the devilish. A man is often almost as much pleased and flattered by his own marriage as he would be by the achievement of what is currently called a seduction. In the one case, as in the other, his emotion is one of triumph. The substitution of pure chance would take away that soothing unction.

The present system, to be sure, also involves chance. Every man realizes it, and even the most bombastic bachelor has moments in which he humbly whispers: "There, but for the grace of God, go I." But that chance has a sugarcoating; it is swathed in egoistic illusion; it shows less stark and intolerable chanciness, so to speak, than the bald hazard of the die. Thus men prefer it, and shrink from the other. In the same way, I have no doubt, the majority of foxes would object to choosing lots to determine the victim of a projected fox-hunt. They prefer to take their chances with the dogs.

23.

Extra-Legal Devices

It is, of course, a rhetorical exaggeration to say that all first-class men escape marriage, and even more of an exaggeration to say that their high qualities go wholly untransmitted to posterity. On the one hand it must be obvious that an appreciable number of them, perhaps by reason of their very detachment and preoccupation, are intrigued into the holy estate, and that not a few of them enter it deliberately, convinced that it is the safest form of liaison possible under Christianity. And on the other hand one must not forget the biological fact that it is quite feasible to achieve offspring without the imprimatur of Church and State. The thing, indeed, is so commonplace that I need not risk a scandal by uncovering it in detail. What I allude to, I need not add, is not that form of irregularity which curses innocent children with the stigma of illegitimacy, but that more refined and thoughtful form which safeguards their social dignity while protecting them against inheritance from their legal fathers. English philosophy, as I have shown, suffers by the fact that Herbert Spencer was too busy to permit himself any such romantic altruism—just as American literature gains enormously by the fact that Walt Whitman adventured, leaving seven sons behind him, three of whom are now well-known American poets and in the forefront of the New Poetry movement.

The extent of this correction of a salient evil of monogamy is very considerable; its operations explain the private disrepute of perhaps a majority of first-rate men; its advantages have been set forth in George Moore's "Euphorion in Texas," though in a clumsy and sentimental way. What is behind it is the profound race sense of women—the instinct which makes them regard the unborn in their every act—perhaps, too, the fact that the interests of the unborn are here identical, as in other situations, with their own egoistic aspirations. As a popular philosopher has shrewdly observed, the objections to polygamy do not come from women, for the average woman is sensible enough to prefer half or a quarter or even a tenth of a first—rate man to the whole devotion of a third—rate man. Considerations of much the same sort also justify polyandry—if not morally, then at least biologically. The average woman, as I have shown, must inevitably view her actual husband with a certain disdain; he is anything but her ideal. In consequence, she cannot help feeling that her children are cruelly handicapped by the fact that he is their father, nor can she help feeling guilty about it; for she knows that he is their father only by reason of her own initiative in the, proceedings anterior to her marriage. If, now, an opportunity presents itself to remove that handicap from at least some of them, and at the same time to realize her ideal and satisfy her vanity—if such a chance offers it is no wonder that she occasionally embraces it.

Here we have an explanation of many lamentable and otherwise inexplicable violations of domestic integrity. The woman in the case is commonly dismissed as vicious, but that is no more than a new example of the common human tendency to attach the concept of viciousness to whatever is natural, and intelligent, and above the comprehension of politicians, theologians and green-grocers.

24.

Intermezzo on Monogamy

The prevalence of monogamy in Christendom is commonly ascribed to ethical motives. This is quite as absurd as ascribing wars to ethical motives which is, of course, frequently done. The simple truth is that ethical motives are no more than deductions from experience, and that they are quickly abandoned whenever experience turns against them. In the present case experience is still overwhelming on the side of monogamy; civilized men are in favour of it because they find that it works. And why does it work? Because it is the most effective of all available antidotes to the alarms and terrors of passion. Monogamy, in brief, kills passion—and passion is the most dangerous of all the surviving enemies to what we call civilization, which is based upon order, decorum, restraint, formality, industry, regimentation. The civilized man—the ideal civilized man—is simply one who never sacrifices the common security to his private passions. He reaches perfection when he even ceases to love passionately—when he reduces the most profound of all his instinctive experience from the level of an ecstasy to the level of a mere device for replenishing armies and workshops of the world, keeping clothes in repair, reducing the infant death-rate, providing enough tenants for every landlord, and making it possible for the Polizei to know where every citizen is at any hour of the day or night. Monogamy accomplishes this, not by producing satiety, but by destroying appetite. It makes passion formal and uninspiring, and so gradually kills it.

The advocates of monogamy, deceived by its moral overtones, fail to get all the advantage out of it that is in it. Consider, for example, the important moral business of safeguarding the virtue of the unmarried—that is, of the still passionate. The present plan in dealing, say, with a young man of twenty, is to surround him with scare-crows and prohibitions—to try to convince him logically that passion is dangerous. This is both supererogation and imbecility—supererogation because he already knows that it is dangerous, and imbecility because it is quite impossible to kill a passion by arguing against it. The way to kill it is to give it rein under unfavourable and dispiriting conditions—to bring it down, by slow stages, to the estate of an absurdity and a horror. How much more, then, could be accomplished if the wild young man were forbidden polygamy, before marriage, but permitted monogamy! The prohibition in this case would be relatively easy to enforce, instead of impossible, as in the other. Curiosity would be satisfied; nature would get out of her cage; even romance would get an inning. Ninety-nine young men out of a hundred would submit, if only because it would be much easier to submit that to resist.

And the result? Obviously, it would be laudable—that is, accepting current definitions of the laudable. The product, after six months, would be a well-regimented and disillusioned young man, as devoid of disquieting and demoralizing, passion as an ancient of eighty—in brief, the ideal citizen of Christendom. The present plan surely fails to produce a satisfactory crop of such ideal citizens. On the one hand its impossible prohibitions cause a multitude of lamentable revolts, often ending in a silly sort of running amok. On the other hand they fill the Y. M. C. A.'s with scared poltroons full of indescribably disgusting Freudian suppressions. Neither group supplies many ideal citizens. Neither promotes the, sort of public morality that is aimed at.

25.

Late Marriages

The marriage of a first-rate man, when it takes place at all, commonly takes place relatively late. He may succumb in the end, but he is almost always able to postpone the disaster a good deal longer than the average poor clodpate, or normal man. If he actually marries early, it is nearly always proof that some intolerable external pressure has been applied to him, as in Shakespeare's case, or that his mental sensitiveness approaches downright insanity, as in Shelley's. This fact, curiously enough, has escaped the observation of an otherwise extremely astute observer, namely Havelock Ellis. In his study of British genius he notes the fact that most men of unusual capacities are the sons of relatively old fathers, but instead of exhibiting the true cause thereof, he ascribes it to a mysterious quality whereby a man already in decline is capable of begetting better offspring than one in full vigour. This is a palpable absurdity, not only because it goes counter to facts long established by animal breeders, but also because it tacitly assumes that talent, and hence the capacity for transmitting it, is an acquired character, and that this character may be transmitted. Nothing could be more unsound. Talent is not an acquired character, but a congenital character, and the man who is born with it has it in early life quite as well as in later life, though Its manifestation may have to wait. James Mill was yet a young man when his son, John Stuart Mill, was born, and not one of his principle books had been written. But though the "Elements of Political Economy" and the "Analysis of the Human Mind" were thus but vaguely formulated in his mind, if they were actually so muchas formulated at all, and it was fifteen years before he wrote them, he was still quite able to transmit the capacity to write them to his son, and that capacity showed itself, years afterward, in the latter's "Principles of Political Economy" and "Essay on Liberty."

But Ellis' faulty inference is still based upon a sound observation, to wit, that the sort of man capable of transmitting high talents to a son is ordinarily a man who does not have a son at all, at least in wedlock, until he has advanced into middle life. The reasons which impel him to yield even then are somewhat obscure, but two or three of them, perhaps, may be vaguely discerned. One lies in the fact that every man, whether of the first-class or of any other class, tends to decline in mental agility as he grows older, though in the actual range and profundity of his intelligence he may keep on improving until he collapses into senility. Obviously, it is mere agility of mind, and not profundity, that is of most value and effect in so tricky and deceptive a combat as the duel of sex. The aging man, with his agility gradually withering, is thus confronted by women in whom it still luxuriates as a function of their relative youth. Not only do women of his own age aspire to ensnare him, but also women of all ages back to adolescence. Hence his average or typical opponent tends to be progressively younger and younger than he is, and in the end the mere advantage of her youth may be sufficient to tip over his tottering defences. This, I take it, is why oldish men are so often intrigued by girls in their teens. It is not that age calls maudlinly to youth, as the poets would have it; it is that age is no match for youth, especially when age is male and youth is female. The case of the late Henrik Ibsen was typical. At forty Ibsen was a sedate family man, and it is doubtful that he ever so much as glanced at a woman; all his thoughts were upon the composition of "The League of Youth," his first social drama. At fifty he was almost as preoccupied; "A Doll's House" was then hatching. But at sixty, with his best work all done and his decline begun, he succumbed preposterously to a flirtatious damsel of eighteen, and thereafter, until actual insanity released him, he mooned like a provincial actor in a sentimental melodrama. Had it not been, indeed, for the fact that he was already married, and to a very sensible wife, he would have run off with this flapper, and so made himself publicly ridiculous.

Another reason for the relatively late marriages of superior men is found, perhaps, in the fact that, as a man grows older, the disabilities he suffers by marriage tend to diminish and the advantages to increase. At thirty aman is terrified by the inhibitions of monogamy and has little taste for the so-called comforts of a home; at sixty he is beyond amorous adventure and is in need of creature ease and security. What he is oftenest conscious of, in these later years, is his physical decay; he sees himself as in imminent danger of falling into neglect and helplessness. He is thus confronted by a choice between getting a wife or hiring a nurse, and he commonly chooses the wife as the less expensive and exacting. The nurse, indeed, would probably try to marry him anyhow; if he employs her in place of a wife he commonly ends by finding himself married and minus a nurse, to his confusion and discomfiture, and to the far greater discomfiture of his heirs and assigns. This process is so obvious and so commonplace that I apologize formally for rehearsing it. What it indicates is simply this: that aman's instinctive aversion to marriage is grounded upon a sense of social and economic self-sufficiency, and that it descends into a mere theory when this self-sufficiency disappears. After all, nature is on the side of mating, and hence on the side of marriage, and vanity is a powerful ally of nature. If men, at the normal mating age, had half as much to gain by marriage as women gain, then, all men would be as ardently in favour of it as women are.

26.

Disparate Unions

This brings us to a fact frequently noted by students of the subject: that first-rate men, when they marry at all, tend to marry noticeably inferior wives. The causes of the phenomenon, so often discussed and so seldom illuminated, should be plain by now. The first-rate man, by postponing marriage as long as possible, often approaches it in the end with his faculties crippled by senility, and is thus open to the advances of women whose attractions are wholly meretricious, e.g., empty flappers, scheming widows, and trained nurses with a highly developed professional technic of sympathy. If he marries at all, indeed, he must commonly marry badly, for women of genuine merit are no longer interested in him; what was once a lodestar is now no more than a smoking smudge. It is this circumstance that account for the low calibre of a good many first-rate men's sons, and gives a certain support to the common notion that they are always third-raters. Those sons inherit from their mothers as well as from their fathers, and the bad strain is often sufficient to obscure and nullify the good strain. Mediocrity, as every Mendelian knows, is a dominant character, and extraordinary ability is recessive character. In a marriage between an able man and a commonplace woman, the chances that any given child will resemble the mother are, roughly speaking, three to one.

The fact suggests the thought that nature is secretly against the superman, and seeks to prevent his birth. We have, indeed, no ground for assuming that the continued progress visualized by man is in actual accord with the great flow of the elemental forces. Devolution is quite as natural as evolution, and may be just as pleasing, or even a good deal more pleasing, to God. If the average man is made in God's image, then a man such as Beethoven or Aristotle is plainly superior to God, and so God may be jealous of him, and eager to see his superiority perish with his bodily frame. All animal breeders know how difficult it is to maintain a fine strain. The universe seems to be in a conspiracy to encourage the endless reproduction of peasants and Socialists, but a subtle and mysterious opposition stands eternally against the reproduction of philosophers.

Per corollary, it is notorious that women of merit frequently marry second-rate men, and bear them children, thus aiding in the war upon progress. One is often astonished to discover that the wife of some sordid and prosaic manufacturer or banker or professional man is a woman of quick intelligence and genuine charm, with intellectual interests so far above his comprehension that he is scarcely so much as aware of them. Again, there are the leading feminists, women artists and other such captains of the sex; their husbands are almost always inferior men, and sometimes downright fools. But not paupers! Not incompetents in a man's world! Not bad husbands! What we here encounter, of course, is no more than a fresh proof of the sagacity of women. The first-rate woman is a realist. She sees clearly that, in a world dominated by second-rate men, the special capacities of the second-rate man are esteemed above all other capacities and given the highest rewards, and she endeavours to get her share of those rewards by marrying a second-rate man at the to of his class. The first-rate man is an admirable creature; his qualities are appreciated by every intelligent woman; as I have just said, it may be reasonably argued that he is actually superior to God. But his attractions, after a certain point, do not run in proportion to his deserts; beyond that he ceases to be a good husband. Hence the pursuit of him is chiefly maintained, not by women who are his peers, but by women who are his inferiors.

Here we unearth another factor: the fascination of what is strange, the charm of the unlike, hliogabalisme. As Shakespeare has put it, there must be some mystery in love—and there can be no mystery between intellectual equals. I dare say that many a woman marries an inferior man, not primarily because he is a good provider (though it is impossible to imagine her overlooking this), but because his very inferiority interests her, and makes her want to remedy it and mother him. Egoism is in the impulse: it is pleasant to have a feeling of superiority, and to be assured that it can be maintained. If now, that feeling he mingled with sexual curiosity and economic self-interest, it obviously supplies sufficient motivation to account for so natural and banal a thing as a marriage. Perhaps the greatest of all these factors is the mere disparity, the naked strangeness. A woman could not love a man, as the phrase is, who wore skirts and pencilled his eye-brows, and by the same token she would probably find it difficult to love a man who matched perfectly her own sharpness of mind. What she most esteems in marriage, on the psychic plane, is the chance it offers for the exercise of that caressing irony which I have already described. She likes to observe that her man is a fool—dear, perhaps, but none the less damned. Her so-called love for him, even at its highest, is always somewhat pitying and patronizing.

27.

The Charm of Mystery

Monogamous marriage, by its very conditions, tends to break down this strangeness. It forces the two contracting parties into an intimacy that is too persistent and unmitigated; they are in contact at too many points, and too steadily. By and by all the mystery of the relation is gone, and they stand in the unsexed position of brother and sister. Thus that "maximum of temptation" of which Shaw speaks has within itself the seeds of its own decay. A husband begins by kissing a pretty girl, his wife; it is pleasant to have her so handy and so willing. He ends by making machiavellian efforts to avoid kissing the every day sharer of his meals, books, bath towels, pocketbook, relatives, ambitions, secrets, malaises and business: a proceeding about as romantic as having his boots blacked. The thing is too horribly dismal for words. Not all the native sentimentalism of man can overcome the distaste and boredom that get into it. Not all the histrionic capacity of woman can attach any appearance of gusto and spontaneity toit.

An estimable lady psychologist of the American Republic, Mrs. Marion Cox, in a somewhat florid book entitled "Ventures into Worlds," has a sagacious essay upon this subject. She calls the essay "Our Incestuous Marriage," and argues accurately that, once the adventurous descends to the habitual, it takes on an offensive and degrading character. The intimate approach, to give genuine joy, must be a concession, a feat of persuasion, a victory; once it loses that character it loses everything. Such a destructive conversion is effected by the average monogamous marriage. It breaks down all mystery and reserve, for how can mystery and reserve survive the use of the same hot water bag and a joint concern about butter and egg bills? What remains, at least on the husband's side, is esteem—the feeling one, has for an amiable aunt. And confidence—the emotion evoked by a lawyer, a dentist ora fortune-teller. And habit—the thing which makes it possible to eat the same breakfast every day, and to windup one's watch regularly, and to earn a living.

Mrs. Cox, if I remember her dissertation correctly, proposes to prevent this stodgy dephlogistication of marriage by interrupting its course—that is, by separating the parties now and then, so that neither will become too familiar and commonplace to the other. By this means, she, argues, curiosity will be periodically revived, and there will be a chance for personality to expand a cappella, and so each reunion will have in it something of the surprise, the adventure and the virtuous satanry of the honeymoon. The husband will not come back to precisely the same wife that he parted from, and the wife will not welcome precisely the same husband. Even supposing them to have gone on substantially as if together, they will have gone on out of sight and hearing of each other, Thus each will find the other, to some extent at least, a stranger, and hence a bit challenging, and hence a bit charming. The scheme has merit. More, it has been tried often, and with success. It is, indeed, a familiar observation that the happiest couples are those who are occasionally separated, and the fact has been embalmed in the trite maxim that absence makes the heart grow fonder. Perhaps not actually fonder, but at any rate more tolerant, more curious, more eager. Two difficulties, however, stand in the way of the widespread adoption of the remedy. One lies in its costliness: the, average couple cannot afford a double establishment, even temporarily. The other lies in the fact that it inevitably arouses the envy and ill-nature of those who cannot adopt it, and so causes a gabbling of scandal. The world invariably suspects the worst. Let man and wife separate to save their happiness from suffocation in the kitchen, the dining room and the connubial chamber, and it will immediately conclude that the corpse is already laid out in the drawing-room.

28.

Woman as Wife

This boredom of marriage, however, is not nearly so dangerous a menace to the institution as Mrs. Cox, with evangelistic enthusiasm, permits herself to think it is. It bears most harshly upon the wife, who is almost always the more intelligent of the pair; in the case of the husband its pains are usually lightened by that sentimentality with which men dilute the disagreeable, particularly in marriage. Moreover, the average male gets his living by such depressing devices that boredom becomes a sort of natural state to him. A man who spends six or eight hours a day acting as teller in a bank, or sitting upon the bench of a court, or looking to the inexpressibly trivial details of some process of manufacturing, or writing imbecile articles for a newspaper, or managing a tramway, or administering ineffective medicines to stupid and uninteresting patients—a man so engaged during all his hours of labour, which means a normal, typical man, is surely not one to be oppressed unduly by the dull round of domesticity. His wife may bore him hopelessly as mistress, just as any other mistress inevitably bores a man (though surely not so quickly and so painfully as a lover bores a woman), but she is not apt to bore him so badly in her other capacities. What he commonly complains about in her, in truth, is not that she tires him by her monotony, but that she tires him by her variety—not that she is too static, but that she is too dynamic. He is weary when he gets home, and asks only the dull peace of a hog in a comfortable sty. This peace is broken by the greater restlessness of his wife, the fruit of her greater intellectual resilience and curiosity.

Of far more potency as a cause of connubial discord is the general inefficiency of a woman at the business of what is called keeping house—a business founded upon a complex of trivial technicalities. As I have argued at length, women are congenitally less fitted for mastering these technicalities than men; the enterprise always costs them more effort, and they are never able to reinforce mere diligent application with that obtuse enthusiasm which men commonly bring to their tawdry and childish concerns. But in addition to their natural incapacity, there is a reluctance based upon a deficiency in incentive, and deficiency in incentive is due to the maudlin sentimentality with which men regard marriage. In this sentimentality lie the germs of most of the evils which beset the institution in Christendom, and particularly in the United States, where sentiment is always carried to inordinate lengths. Having abandoned the mediaeval concept of woman as temptress the men of the Nordic race have revived the correlative mediaeval concept of woman as angel and to bolster up that character they have create for her a vast and growing mass of immunities culminating of late years in the astounding doctrine that, under the contract of marriage, all the duties lie upon the man and all the privileges appertain to the woman. In part this doctrine has been established by the intellectual enterprise and audacity of woman. Bit by bit, playing upon masculine stupidity, sentimentality and lack of strategical sense, they have formulated it, developed it, and entrenched it in custom and law. But in other part it is the plain product of the donkeyish vanity which makes almost every man view the practical incapacity of his wife as, in some vague way, a tribute to his own high mightiness and consideration. Whatever is revolt against her immediate indolence and efficiency, his ideal is nearly always a situation in which she will figure as a magnificent drone, a sort of empress without portfolio, entirely discharged from every unpleasant labour and responsibility.

29.

Marriage and the Law

This was not always the case. No more than a century ago, even by American law, the most sentimental in the world, the husband was the head of the family firm, lordly and autonomous. He had authority over the purse-strings, over the children, and even over his wife. He could enforce his mandates by appropriate punishment, including the corporal. His sovereignty and dignity were carefully guarded by legislation, the product of thousands of years of experience and ratiocination. He was safeguarded in his self-respect by the most elaborate and efficient devices, and they had the support of public opinion.

Consider, now, the changes that a few short years have wrought. Today, by the laws of most American states—laws proposed, in most cases, by maudlin and often notoriously extravagant agitators, and passerby sentimental orgy—all of the old rights of the husband have been converted into obligations. He no longer has any control over his wife's property; she may devote its income to the family or she may squander that income upon idle follies, and he can do nothing. She has equal authority in regulating and disposing of the children, and in the case of infants, more than he. There is no law compelling her to do her share of the family labour: she may spend her whole time in cinema theatres or gadding about the shops an she will. She cannot be forced to perpetuate the family name if she does not want to. She cannot be attacked with masculine weapons, e.g., fists and firearms, when she makes an assault with feminine weapons, e.g.,snuffling, invective and sabotage. Finally, no lawful penalty can be visited upon her if she fails absolutely, either deliberately or through mere incapacity, to keep the family habitat clean, the children in order, and the victuals eatable.

Now view the situation of the husband. The instant he submits to marriage, his wife obtains a large and inalienable share in his property, including all he may acquire in future; in most American states the minimum is one-third, and, failing children, one-half. He cannot dispose of his real estate without her consent; He cannot even deprive her of it by will. She may bring up his children carelessly and idiotically, cursing them with abominable manners and poisoning their nascent minds against him, and he has no redress. She may neglect her home, gossip and lounge about all day, put impossible food upon his table, steal his small change, pry into his private papers, hand over his home to the Periplaneta americana, accuse him falsely of preposterous adulteries, affront his'friends, and lie about him to the neighbours—and he can do nothing. She may compromise his honour by indecent dressing, write letters to moving-picture actors, and expose him to ridicule by going into politics—and he is helpless.

Let him undertake the slightest rebellion, over and beyond mere rhetorical protest, and the whole force of the state comes down upon him. If he corrects her with the bastinado or locks her up, he is good for six months in jail. If he cuts off her revenues, he is incarcerated until he makes them good. And if he seeks surcease in flight, taking the children with him, he is pursued by the gendarmerie, brought back to his duties, and depicted in the public press as a scoundrelly kidnapper, fit only for the knout. In brief, she is under no legal necessity whatsoever to carry out her part of the compact at the altar of God, whereas he faces instant disgrace and punishment for the slightest failure to observe its last letter. For a few grave crimes of commission, true enough, she may be proceeded against. Open adultery is a recreation that is denied to her. She cannot poison her husband. She must not assault him with edged tools, or leave him altogether, or strip off her few remaining garments and go naked. But for the vastly more various and numerous crimes of omission—and in sum they are more exasperating and intolerable than even overt felony—she cannot be brought to book at all.

The scene I depict is American, but it will soon extend its horrors to all Protestant countries. The newly enfranchised women of every one of them cherish long programs of what they call social improvement, and practically the whole of that improvement is based upon devices for augmenting their own relative autonomy and power. The English wife of tradition, so thoroughly a femme covert, is being displaced by a gadabout, truculent, irresponsible creature, full of strange new ideas about her rights, and strongly disinclined to submit to her husband's authority, or to devote herself honestly to the upkeep of his house, or to bear him a biological sufficiency of heirs. And the German Hausfrau, once so innocently consecrated to Kirche, Kche und Kinder, is going the same way.

30.

The Emancipated Housewife

What has gone on in the United States during the past two generations is full of lessons and warnings for the rest of the world. The American housewife of an earlier day was famous for her unremitting diligence. She not only cooked, washed and ironed; she also made shift to master such more complex arts as spinning, baking and brewing. Her expertness, perhaps, never reached a high level, but at all events she made a gallant effort. But that was long, long ago, before the new enlightenment rescued her. Today, in her average incarnation, she is not only incompetent (alack, as I have argued, rather beyond her control) ; she is also filled with the notion that a conscientious discharge of her few remaining duties is, in some vague way, discreditable and degrading. To call her a good cook, I daresay, was never anything but flattery; the early American cuisine was probably a fearful thing, indeed. But today the flattery turns into a sort of libel, and she resents it, or, at all events, does not welcome it. I used to know an American literary man, educated on the Continent, who married a woman because she had exceptional gifts in this department. Years later, at one of her dinners, a friend of her husband's tried to please her by mentioning the fact, to which be had always been privy. But instead of being complimented, as a man might have been if told that his wife had married him because be was a good lawyer, or surgeon, or blacksmith, this unusual housekeeper, suffering a renaissance of usualness, denounced the guest as a liar, ordered him out of the house, and threatened to leave her husband.

This disdain of offices that, after all, are necessary, and might as well be faced with some show of cheerfulness, takes on the character of a definite cult in the United States, and the stray woman who attends to them faithfully is laughed at as a drudge and a fool, just as she is apt to be dismissed as a "brood sow" (I quote literally, craving absolution for the phrase: a jury of men during the late war, on very thin patriotic grounds, jailed the author of it) if she favours her lord with viable issue. One result is the notorious villainousness of American cookery—a villainousness so painful to a cultured uvula that a French hack-driver, if his wife set its masterpieces before him, would brain her with his linoleum hat. To encounter a decent meal in an American home of the middle class, simple, sensibly chosen and competently cooked, becomes almost as startling as to meet a Y. M.C. A. secretary in a bordello, and a good deal rarer. Such a thing, in most of the large cities of the Republic, scarcely has any existence. If the average American husband wants a sound dinner he must go to a restaurant to get it, just as if he wants to refresh himself with the society of charming and well-behaved children, he has to go to an orphan asylum. Only the immigrant can take his case and invite his soul within his own house.

IV

Woman Suffrage

31.

The Crowning Victory

It is my sincere hope that nothing I have here exhibited will be mistaken by the nobility and gentry for moral indignation. No such feeling, in truth, is in my heart. Moral judgments, as old Friedrich used to say, are foreign to my nature. Setting aside the vast herd which shows no definable character at all, it seems to me that the minority distinguished by what is commonly regarded as an excess of sin is very much more admirable than the minority distinguished by an excess of virtue. My experience of the world has taught me that the average wine-bibber is a far better fellow than the, average prohibitionist, and that the average rogue is better company than the average poor drudge, and that the worst white, slave trader of my acquaintance is a decenter man than the best vice crusader. In the same way I am convinced that the average woman, whatever her deficiencies, is greatly superior to the average man. The very ease with which she defies and swindles him in several capital situations of life is the clearest of proofs of her general superiority. She did not obtain her present high immunities as a gift from the gods, but only after a long and often bitter fight, and in that fight she exhibited forensic and tactical talents of a truly admirable order. There was no weakness of man that she did not penetrate and take advantage of. There was no trick that she did not put to effective use. There was no device so bold and inordinate that it daunted her.

The latest and greatest fruit of this feminine talent for combat is the extension of the suffrage, now universal in the Protestant countries, and even advancing in those of the Greek and Latin rites. This fruit was garnered, not by an, attack en masse, but by a mere foray. I believe that the majority of women, for reasons that I shall presently expose, were not eager for the extension, and regard it as of small value today. They know that they can get what they want without going to the actual polls for it; moreover, they are out of sympathy with most of the brummagem reforms advocated by the professional suffragists, male and female. The mere statement of the current suffragist platform, with its long list of quack sure-cures for all the sorrows of the world, is enough to make them smile sadly. In particular, they are sceptical of all reforms that depend upon the mass action of immense numbers of voters, large sections of whom are wholly devoid of sense. A normal woman, indeed, no more believes in democracy in the nation than she believes in democracy at her own fireside; she knows that there must be a class to order and a class to obey, and that the two can never coalesce. Nor is she, susceptible to the stock sentimentalities upon which the whole democratic process is based. This was shown very dramatically in them United States at the national election of 1920, in which the late Woodrow Wilson was brought down to colossal and ignominious defeat—The first general election in which all American women could vote. All the sentimentality of the situation was on the side of Wilson, and yet fully three-fourths of the newly-enfranchised women voters voted against him. He is, despite his talents for deception, a poor popular psychologist, and so he made an inept effort to fetch the girls by tear-squeezing: every connoisseur will remember his bathos about breaking the heart of the world. Well, very few women believe in broken hearts, and the cause is not far to seek: practically every woman above the, age of twenty-five has a broken heart. That is to say, she has been vastly disappointed, either by failing to nab some pretty fellow that her heart was set on, or, worse, by actually nabbing him, and then discovering him to be a bounder or an imbecile, or both. Thus walking the world with broken hearts, women know that the injury is not serious. When he pulled out the Vox angelica stop and began sobbing and snuffling and blowing his nose tragically, the learned doctor simply drove all the women voters into the arms of the Hon. Warren Gamaliel Harding, who was too stupid to invent any issues at all, but simply took negative advantage of the distrust aroused by his opponent.

Once the women of Christendom become at ease in the use of the ballot, and get rid of the preposterous harridans who got it for them and who now seek to tell them what to do with it, they will proceed to a scotching of many of the sentimentalities which currently corrupt politics. For one thing, I believe that they will initiate measures against democracy—the worst evil of the present-day world. When they come to the matter, they will certainly not ordain the extension of the suffrage to children, criminals and the insane in brief, to those ever more inflammable and knavish than the male hinds who have enjoyed it for so long; they will try to bring about its restriction, bit by bit, to the small minority that is intelligent, agnostic and self-possessed—say six women to one man. Thus, out of their greater instinct for reality, they will make democracy safe for a democracy.

The curse of man, and the cause of nearly all his woes, is his stupendous capacity for believing the incredible. He is forever embracing delusions, and each new one is worse than all hat have gone before. But where is the delusion that women cherish—I mean habitually, firmly, passionately? Who will draw up a list of propositions, held and maintained by them in sober earnest, that are obviously not true? (I allude here, of course, to genuine women, not to suffragettes and other such pseudo-males). As for me, I should not like to undertake such a list. I know of nothing, in fact, that properly belongs to it. Women, as a class, believe in none of the ludicrous rights, duties and pious obligations that men are forever gabbling about. Their superior intelligence is in no way more eloquently demonstrated than by their ironical view of all such phantasmagoria. Their habitual attitude toward men is one of aloof disdain, and their habitual attitude toward what men believe in, and get into sweats about, and bellow for, is substantially the same, It takes twice as long to convert a body of women to some new fallacy as it takes to convert a body of men, and even then they halt, hesitate and are full of mordant criticisms. The women of Colorado had been voting for 21 years before they succumbed to prohibition sufficiently to allow the man voters of the state to adopt it; their own majority voice was against it to the end. During the interval the men voters of a dozen non-suffrage American states had gone shrieking to the mourners' bench. In California, enfranchised in 1911, the women rejected the dry revelation in 1914. National prohibition was adopted during the war without their votes—they did not get the franchise throughout the country until it was in the Constitution—and it is without their support today. The American man, despite his reputation for lawlessness, is actually very much afraid of the police, and in all the regions where prohibition is now actually enforced he makes excuses for his poltroonish acceptance of it by arguing that it will do him good in the long run, or that he ought to sacrifice his private desires to the common weal. But it is almost impossible to find an American woman of any culture who is in favour of it. One and all, they are opposed to the turmoil and corruption that it involves, and resentful'of the invasion of liberty underlying it. Being realists, they have no belief in any program which proposes to cure the natural swinishness of men by legislation. Every normal woman believes, and quite accurately, that the average man is very much like her husband, John, and she knows very well that John is a weak, silly and knavish fellow, and that any effort to convert him into an archangel overnight is bound to come to grief. As for her view of the average creature of her own sex, it is marked by a cynicism so penetrating and so destructive that a clear statement of it would shock beyond endurance.

32.

The Woman Voter

Thus there is not the slightest chance that the enfranchised women of Protestantdom, once they become at ease in the use of the ballot, will give, any heed to the ex-suffragettes who now presume to lead and instruct them in politics. Years ago I predicted that these suffragettes, tried out by victory, would turn out to be idiots. They are now hard at work proving it. Half of them devote themselves to advocating reforms, chiefly of a sexual character, so utterly preposterous that even male politicians and newspaper editors laugh at them; the other half succumb absurdly to the blandishments of the old-time male politicians, and so enroll themselves in the great political parties. A woman who joins one of these parties simply becomes an imitation man, which is to say, a donkey. Thereafter she is nothing but an obscure cog in an ancient and creaking machine, the sole intelligible purpose of which is to maintain a horde of scoundrels in public office. Her vote is instantly set off by the vote of some sister who joins the other camorra. Parenthetically, I may add that all of the ladies to take to this political immolation seem to me to be frightfully plain. I know those of England, Germany and Scandinavia only by their portraits in the illustrated papers, but those of the United States I have studied at close range at various large political gatherings, including the two national conventions first following the extension of the suffrage. I am surely no fastidious fellow—in fact, I prefer a certain melancholy decay in women to the loud, circus-wagon brilliance of youth—but I give you my word that there were not five women at either national convention who could have embraced me in camera without first giving me chloral. Some of the chief stateswomen on show, in fact, were so downright hideous that I felt faint every time I had to look at them.

The reform-monging suffragists seem to be equally devoid of the more caressing gifts. They may be filled with altruistic passion, but they certainly have bad complexions, and not many of them know how to dress their hair. Nine-tenths of them advocate reforms aimed at the alleged lubricity of the male-the single standard, medical certificates for bridegrooms, birth-control, and so on. The motive here, I believe, is mere rage and jealousy. The woman who is not pursued sets up the doctrine that pursuit is offensive to her sex, and wants to make it a felony. No genuinely attractive woman has any such desire. She likes masculine admiration, however violently expressed, and is quite able to take care of herself. More, she is well aware that very few men are bold enough to offer it without a plain invitation, and this awareness makes her extremely cynical of all women who complain of being harassed, beset, storied, and seduced. All the more intelligent women that I know, indeed, are unanimously of the opinion that no girl in her right senses has ever been actually seduced since the world began; whenever they bear of a case, they sympathize with the man. Yet more, the normal woman of lively charms, roving about among men, always tries to draw the admiration of those who have previously admired elsewhere; she prefers the professional to the amateur, and estimates her skill by the attractiveness of the huntresses who have hitherto stalked it. The iron-faced suffragist propagandist, if she gets a man at all, must get one wholly without sentimental experience. If he has any, her crude manoeuvres make him laugh and he is repelled by her lack of pulchritude and amiability. All such suffragists(save a few miraculous beauties) marry ninth-rate men when they marry at all. They have to put up with the sort of castoffs who are almost ready to fall in love with lady physicists, embryologists, and embalmers.

Fortunately for the human race, the campaigns of these indignant viragoes will come to naught. Men will keep on pursuing women until hell freezes over, and women will keep luring them on. If the latter enterprise were abandoned, in fact, the whole game of love would play out, for not many men take any notice of women spontaneously. Nine men out of ten would be quite happy, I believe, if there were no women in the world, once they had grown accustomed to the quiet. Practically all men are their happiest when they are engaged upon activities—for example, drinking, gambling, hunting, business, adventure—to which women are not ordinarily admitted. It is women who seduce them from such celibate doings. The hare postures and gyrates in front of the hound. The way to put an end to the gaudy crimes that the suffragist alarmists talk about is to shave the heads of all the pretty girls in the world, and pluck out their eyebrows, and pull their teeth, and put them in khaki, and forbid them to wriggle on dance-floors, or to wear scents, or to use lip-sticks, or to roll their eyes. Reform, as usual, mistakes the fish for the fly.

33.

A Glance Into the Future

The present public prosperity of the ex-suffragettes is chiefly due to the fact that the old-time male politicians, being naturally very stupid, mistake them for spokesmen for the whole body of women, and so show them politeness. But soon or late—and probably disconcertingly soon—the great mass of sensible and agnostic women will turn upon them and depose them, and thereafter the woman vote will be no longer at the disposal of bogus Great Thinkers and messiahs. If the suffragettes continue to fill the newspapers with nonsense, once that change has been effected, it will be only as a minority sect of tolerated idiots, like the Swedenborgians, Christian Scientists, Seventh Day Adventists and other such fanatics of today. This was the history of the extension of the suffrage in all of the American states that made it before the national enfranchisement of women and it will be repeated in the nation at large, and in Great Britain and on the Continent. Women are not taken in by quackery as readily as men are; the hardness of their shell of logic makes it difficult to penetrate to their emotions. For one woman who testifies publicly that she has been cured of cancer by some swindling patent medicine, there are at least twenty masculine witnesses. Even such frauds as the favourite American elixir, Lydia Pinkham's Vegetable Compound, which are ostensibly remedies for specifically feminine ills, anatomically impossible in the male, are chiefly swallowed, so an intelligent druggist tells me, by men.

My own belief, based on elaborate inquiries and long meditation, is that the grant of the ballot to women marks the concealed but none the less real beginning of an improvement in our politics, and, in the end, in our whole theory of government. As things stand, an intelligent grappling with some of the capital problems of the commonwealth is almost impossible. A politician normally prospers under democracy, not in proportion as his principles are sound and his honour incorruptible, but in proportion a she excels in the manufacture of sonorous phrases, and the invention of imaginary perils and imaginary defences against them. Our politics thus degenerates into a mere pursuit of hobgoblins; the male voter, a coward as well as an ass, is forever taking fright at a new one and electing some mountebank to lay it. For a hundred years past the people of the United States, the most terrible existing democratic state, have scarcely had apolitical campaign that was not based upon some preposterous fear—first of slavery and then of the manumitted slave, first of capitalism and then of communism, first of the old and then of the novel. It is a peculiarity of women that they are not easily set off by such alarms, that they do not fall readily into such facile tumults and phobias. What starts a male meeting to snuffling and trembling most violently is precisely the thing that would cause a female meeting to sniff. What we need, to ward off mobocracy and safeguard a civilized form of government, is more of this sniffing. What we need—and in the end it must come—is a sniff so powerful that it will call a halt upon the, navigation of the ship from the forecastle, and put a competent staff on the bridge, and lay a course that is describable in intelligible terms.

The officers nominated by the male electorate in modern democracies before the extension of the suffrage were, usually chosen, not for their competence but for their mere talent for idiocy; they reflected accurately thymol weakness for whatever is rhetorical and sentimental and feeble and untrue. Consider, for example, what happened in a salient case. Every four years the male voters of the United States chose from among themselves one who was put forward as the man most fit, of all resident men, to be the first citizen of the commonwealth. He was chosen after interminable discussion; his qualifications were thoroughly canvassed; very large powers and dignities were put into his hands. Well, what did we commonly find when we examined this gentleman? We found, not a profound thinker, not a leader of sound opinion, not a man of notable sense, but merely a wholesaler of notions so infantile that they must needs disgust a sentient suckling—in brief, a spouting geyser of fallacies and sentimentalities, a cataract of unsupported assumptions and hollow moralizings, a tedious phrase-merchant and platitudinarian, a fellow whose noblest flights of thought were flattered when they were called comprehensible—specifically, a Wilson, a Taft, a Roosevelt, or a Harding.

This was the male champion. I do not venture upon the cruelty of comparing his bombastic flummeries to the clear reasoning of a woman of like fame and position; all I ask of you is that you weigh them, for sense, for shrewdness, for intelligent grasp of obscure relations, for intellectual honesty and courage, with the ideas of the average midwife.

34.

The Suffragette

I have spoken with some disdain of the suffragette. What is the matter with her, fundamentally, is simple: she is a woman who has stupidly carried her envy of certain of the superficial privileges of men to such a point that it takes on the character of an obsession, and makes her blind to their valueless and often chiefly imaginary character. In particular, she centres this frenzy of hers upon one definite privilege, to wit, the alleged privilege of promiscuity in amour, the modern droit du seigneur. Read the books of the chief lady Savonarolas, and you will find running through them an hysterical denunciation of what is called the double standard of morality; there is, indeed, a whole literature devoted exclusively to it. The existence of this double standard seems to drive the poor girls half frantic. They bellow raucously for its abrogation, and demand that the frivolous male be visited with even more idiotic penalties than those which now visit the aberrant female; some even advocate gravely his mutilation by surgery, that he may be forced into rectitude by a physical disability for sin.

All this, of course, is hocus-pocus, and the judicious are not deceived by it for an instant. What these virtuous bel dames actually desire in their hearts is not that the male be reduced to chemical purity, but that the franchise of dalliance be extended to themselves. The most elementary acquaintance with Freudian psychology exposes their secret animus. Unable to ensnare males under the present system, or at all events, unable to ensnare males sufficiently appetizing to arouse the envy of other women, they leap to the theory that it would be easier if the rules were less exacting. This theory exposes their deficiency in the chief character of their sex: accurate observation. The fact is that, even if they possessed the freedom that men are supposed to possess, they would still find it difficult to achieve their ambition, for the average man, whatever his stupidity, is at least keen enough in judgment to prefer a single wink from a genuinely attractive woman to the last delirious favours of the typical suffragette. Thus the theory of the whoopers and snorters of the cause, in its esoteric as well as in its public aspect, is unsound. They are simply women who, in their tastes and processes of mind, are two-thirds men, and the fact explains their failure to achieve presentable husbands, or even consolatory betrayal, quite as effectively as it explains the ready credence they give to political an philosophical absurdities.

35.

A Mythical Dare-Devil

The truth is that the picture of male carnality that such women conjure up belongs almost wholly to fable, as I have already observed in dealing with the sophistries of Dr. Eliza Burt Gamble, a paralogist on a somewhat higher plane. As they depict him in their fevered treatises on illegitimacy, white-slave trading and ophthalmia neonatorum, the average male adult of the Christian and cultured countries leads a life of gaudy lubricity, rolling magnificently from one liaison to another, and with an almost endless queue of ruined milliners, dancers, charwomen, parlour-maids and waitresses behind him, all dying of poison and despair. The life of man, as these furiously envious ones see it, is the life of a leading actor in a boulevard revue. He is a polygamous, multigamous, myriadigamous; an insatiable and unconscionable debauche, a monster of promiscuity; prodigiously unfaithful to his wife, and even to his friends' wives; fathomlessly libidinous and superbly happy.

Needless to say, this picture bears no more relation to the facts than a dissertation on major strategy by a military "expert" promoted from dramatic critic. If the chief suffragette scare mongers (I speak without any embarrassing naming of names) were attractive enough to men to get near enough to enough men to know enough about them for their purpose they would paralexia the Dorcas societies with no such cajoling libels. As a matter of sober fact, the average man of our time and race is quite incapable of all these incandescent and intriguing divertisements. He is far more virtuous than they make him out, far less schooled in sin far less enterprising and ruthless. I do not say, of course, that he is pure in heart, for the chances are that he isn't; what I do say is that, in the overwhelming majority of cases, he is pure in act, even in the face of temptation. And why? For several main reasons, not to go into minor ones. One is that he lacks the courage. Another is that he lacks the money. Another is that he is fundamentally moral, and has a conscience. It takes more sinful initiative than he has in him to plunge into any affair save the most casual and sordid; it takes more ingenuity and intrepidity than he has in him to carry it off; it takes more money than he can conceal from his consort to finance it. A man may force his actual wife to share the direst poverty, but even the least vampirish woman of the third part demands to be courted in what, considering his station in life, is the grand manner, and the expenses of that grand manner scare off all save a small minority of specialists in deception. So long, indeed, as a wife knows her husband's in come accurately, she has a sure means of holding him to his oaths.

Even more effective than the fiscal barrier is the barrier of poltroonery. The one character that distinguishes man from the other higher vertebrate, indeed, is his excessive timorousness, his easy yielding to alarms, his incapacity for adventure without a crowd behind him. In his normal incarnation he is no more capable of initiating an extra-legal affair—at all events, above the mawkish harmlessness of a flirting match with a cigar girl in a cafe-than he is of scaling the battlements of hell. He likes to think of himself doing it, just as he likes to think of himself leading a cavalry charge or climbing the Matterhorn. Often, indeed, his vanity leads him to imagine the thing done, and he admits by winks and blushes that he is a bad one. But at the bottom of all that tawdry pretence there is usually nothing more material than an oafish smirk at some disgusted shop-girl, or a scraping of shins under the table. Let any woman who is disquieted by reports of her husband's derelictions figure to herself how long it would have taken him to propose to her if left to his own enterprise, and then let her ask herself if so pusillanimous a creature could be imaged in the role of Don Giovanni.

Finally, there is his conscience—the accumulated sediment of ancestral faintheartedness in countless generations, with vague religious fears and superstitions to leaven and mellow it. What! a conscience? Yes, dear friends, a conscience. That conscience may be imperfect, inept, unintelligent, brummagem. It may be indistinguishable, at times, from the mere fear that someone may be looking. It may be shot through with hypocrisy, stupidity, play-acting. But nevertheless, as consciences go in Christendom, it is genuinely entitled to the name—and it is always in action. A man, remember, is not a being in vacuo; he is the fruit and slave of the environment that bathes him. One cannot enter the House of Commons, the United States Senate, or a prison for felons without becoming, in some measure, a rascal. One cannot fall overboard without shipping water. One cannot pass through a modern university without carrying away scars. And by the same token one cannot live and have one's being in a modern democratic state, year in and year out, without falling, to some extent at least, under that moral obsession which is the hall-mark of the mob-man set free. A citizen of such astate, his nose buried in Nietzsche, "Man and Superman," and other such advanced literature, may caress himself with the notion that he is an immoralist, that his soul is full of soothing sin, that he has cut himself loose from the revelation of God. But all the while there is a part of him that remains a sound Christian, a moralist, a right thinking and forward-looking man. And that part, in times of stress, asserts itself. It may not worry him on ordinary occasions. It may not stop him when he swears, or takes a nip of whiskey behind the door, or goes motoring on Sunday; it may even let him alone when he goes to a leg-show. But the moment a concrete Temptress rises before him, her noses now-white, her lips rouged, her eyelashes drooping provokingly—the moment such an abandoned wench has at him, and his lack of ready funds begins to conspire with his lack of courage to assault and wobble him—at that precise moment his conscience flares into function, and so finishes his business. First he sees difficulty, then he sees the danger, then he sees wrong. The result is that he slinks off in trepidation, and another vampire is baffled of her prey.

It is, indeed, the secret scandal of Christendom, at least in the Protestant regions, that most men are faithful to their wives. You will a travel a long way before you find a married man who will admit that he is, but the facts are the facts, and I am surely not one to flout them.

36.

The Origin of a Delusion

The origin of the delusion that the average man is a Leopold II or Augustus the Strong, with the amorous experience of a guinea pig, is not far to seek. It lies in three factors, the which I rehearse briefly:

1. The idiotic vanity of men, leading to their eternal boasting, either by open lying or sinister hints.
2 .The notions of vice crusaders, nonconformist divines, Y. M.C. A. secretaries, and other such libidinous poltroons as to what they would do themselves if they bad the courage.
3. The ditto of certain suffragettes as to ditto.

Here you have the genesis of a generalization that gives the less critical sort of women a great deal of needless uneasiness and vastly augments the natural conceit of men. Some pornographic old fellow, in the discharge, of his duties as director of an anti-vice society, puts in an evening ploughing through such books as "The Memoirs of Fanny Hill," Casanova's Confessions, the Cena Trimalchionis of Gaius Petronius, and II Samuel. From this perusal he arises with the conviction that life amid the red lights must be one stupendous whirl of deviltry, that the clerks he sees in Broadway or Piccadilly at night are out for revels that would have caused protests in Sodom and Nineveh, that the average man who chooses hell leads an existence comparable to that of a Mormon bishop, that the world outside the Bible class is packed like a sardine-can with betrayed salesgirls, that every man who doesn't believe that Jonah swallowed the whale spends his whole leisure leaping through the seventh hoop of the Decalogue. "If I were not saved and anointed of God," whispers the vice director into his own ear, "that is what I, the Rev. Dr. Jasper Barebones, would be doing. The late King David did it; he was human, and hence immoral. The late King Edward VII was not beyond suspicion: the very numeral in his name has its suggestions. Millions of others go the same route . . . Ergo, Up, guards, and at'em! Bring me the pad of blank warrants! Order out the seachlights and scaling-ladders! Swear in four hundred more policemen! Let us chase these hell-hounds out of Christendom, and make the world safe for monogamy, poor working girls, and infant damnation!"

Thus the hound of heaven, arguing fallaciously from his own secret aspirations. Where he makes his mistake is in assuming that the unconsecrated, while sharing his longing to debauch and betray, are free from his other weaknesses, e.g., his timidity, his lack of resourcefulness, his conscience. As I have said, they are not. The vast majority of those who appear in the public haunts of sin are there, not to engage in overt acts of ribaldry, but merely to tremble agreeably upon the edge of the abyss. They are the same skittish experimentalists, precisely, who throng the midway at a world's fair, and go to smutty shows, and take in sex magazines, and read the sort of books that our vice crusading friend reads. They like to conjure up the charms of carnality, and to help out their somewhat sluggish imaginations by actual peeps at it, but when it comes to taking a forthright header into the sulphur they usually fail to muster up the courage. For one clerk who succumbs to the houris of the pave, there are five hundred who succumb to lack of means, the warnings of the sex hygienists, and their own depressing consciences. For one "clubman"—i.e., bagman or suburban vestryman—who invades the women's shops, engages the affection of some innocent miss, lures her into infamy and then sells her to the Italians, there are one thousand who never get any further than asking the price of cologne water and discharging a few furtive winks. And for one husband of the Nordic race who maintains a blonde chorus girl in oriental luxury around the comer, there are ten thousand who are as true to their wives, year in and year out, as so many convicts in the death-house, and would be no more capable of any such loathsome malpractice, even in the face of free opportunity, than they would be of cutting off the ears of their young.

I am sorry to blow up so much romance. In particular, I am sorry for the suffragettes who specialize in the double standard, for when they get into pantaloons at last, and have the new freedom, they will discover to their sorrow that they have been pursuing a chimera—that there is really no such animal as the male anarchist they have been denouncing and envying—that the wholesale fornication of man, at least under Christian democracy, has little more actual existence than honest advertising or sound cooking. They have followed the porno maniacs in embracing a piece of buncombe, and when the day of deliverance comes it will turn to ashes in their arms.

Their error, as I say, lies in overestimating the courage and enterprise of man. They themselves, barring mere physical valour, a quality in which the average man is far exceeded by the average jackal or wolf, have more of both. If the consequences, to a man, of the slightest descent from virginity were one-tenth as swift and barbarous as the consequences to a young girl in like case, it would take a division of infantry to dredge up a single male flouter of that lex talionis in the whole western world. As things stand today, even with the odds so greatly in his favour, the average male hesitates and is thus not lost. Turn to the statistics of the vice crusaders if you doubt it. They show that the weekly receipts of female recruits upon the wharves of sin are always more than the demand; that more young women enter upon the vermilion career than can make respectable livings at it; that the pressure of the temptation they hold out is the chief factor in corrupting our undergraduates. What was the first act of the American Army when it began summoning its young clerks and college boys and plough hands to conscription camps? Its first act was to mark off a so-called moral zone around each camp, and to secure it with trenches and machine guns, and to put a lot of volunteer termagants to patrolling it, that the assembled jeunesse might be protected in their rectitude from the immoral advances of the adjacent milkmaids and poor working girls.

37.

Women as Martyrs

I have given three reasons for the prosperity of the notion that man is a natural polygamist, bent eternally upon fresh dives into Lake of Brimstone No. 7. To these another should be added: the thirst for martyrdom which shows itself in so many women, particularly under the higher forms of civilization. This unhealthy appetite, in fact, may be described as one of civilization's diseases; it is almost unheard of in more primitive societies. The savage woman, unprotected by her rude culture and forced to heavy and incessant labour, has retained her physical strength and with it her honesty and self-respect. The civilized woman, gradually degenerated by a greater ease, and helped down that hill by the pretensions of civilized man, has turned her infirmity into a virtue, and so affects a feebleness that is actually far beyond the reality. It is by this route that she can most effectively disarm masculine distrust, and get what she wants. Man is flattered by any acknowledgment, however insincere, of his superior strength and capacity. He likes to be leaned upon, appealed to, followed docilely. And this tribute to his might caresses him on the psychic plane as well as on the plane of the obviously physical. He not only enjoys helping a woman over a gutter; he also enjoys helping her dry her tears. The result is the vast pretence that characterizes the relations of the sexes under civilization—the double pretence of man's cunning and autonomy and of woman's dependence and deference. Man is always looking for someone to boast to; woman is always looking for a shoulder to put her head on.

This feminine affectation, of course, has gradually taken on the force of a fixed habit, and so it has got a certain support, by a familiar process of self-delusion, in reality. The civilized woman inherits that habit as she inherits her cunning. She is born half convinced that she is really as weak and helpless as she later pretends to be, and the prevailing folklore offers her endless corroboration. One of the resultant phenomena is the delight in martyrdom that one so often finds in women, and particularly in the least alert and introspective of them. They take a heavy, unhealthy pleasure in suffering; it subtly pleases them to be bard put upon; they like to picture themselves as slaughtered saints. Thus they always find something to complain of; the very conditions of domestic life give them a superabundance of clinical material. And if, by any chance, such material shows a falling off, they are uneasy and unhappy. Let a woman have a husband whose conduct is not reasonably open to question, and she will invent mythical offences to make him bearable. And if her invention fails she will be plunged into the utmost misery and humiliation. This fact probably explains many mysterious divorces: the husband was not too bad, but too good. For public opinion among women, remember, does not favour the woman who is full of a placid contentment and has no masculine torts to report; if she says that her husband is wholly satisfactory she is looked upon as a numskull even more dense that he is himself. A man, speaking of his wife to other men, always praises her extravagantly. Boasting about her soothes his vanity; he likes to stir up the envy of his fellows. But when two women talk of their husbands it is mainly atrocities that they describe. The most esteemed woman gossip is the one with the longest and most various repertoire of complaints.

This yearning for martyrdom explains one of the commonly noted characters of women: their eager flair for bearing physical pain. As we have seen, they have actually a good deal less endurance than men; massive injuries shock them more severely and kill them more quickly. But when acute algesia is unaccompanied by any profounder phenomena they are undoubtedly able to bear it with a far greater show of resignation. The reason is not far to seek. In pain a man sees only an invasion of his liberty, strength and self-esteem. It floors him, masters him, and makes him ridiculous. But a woman, more subtle and devious in her processes of mind, senses the dramatic effect that the spectacle of her suffering makes upon the spectators, already filled with compassion for her feebleness. She would thus much rather be praised for facing pain with a martyr's fortitude than for devising some means of getting rid of it the first thought of a man. No woman could have invented chloroform, nor, for that matter, alcohol. Both drugs offer an escape from situations and experiences that, even in aggravated forms, women relish. The woman who drinks as men drink—that is, to raise her threshold of sensation and ease the agony of living—nearly always shows a deficiency in feminine characters and an undue preponderance of masculine characters. Almost invariably you will find her vain and boastful, and full of other marks of that bombastic exhibitionism which is so sterlingly male.

38.

Pathological Effects

This feminine craving for martyrdom, of course, often takes on a downright pathological character, and so engages the psychiatrist. Women show many other traits of the same sort. To be a woman under our Christian civilization, indeed, means to live a life that is heavy with repression and dissimulation, and this repression and dissimulation, in the long run, cannot fail to produce effects that are indistinguishable from disease. You will find some of them described at length in any handbook on psychoanalysis. The Viennese, Adler, and the Dane, Poul Bjerre, argue, indeed, that womanliness itself, as it is encountered under Christianity, is a disease. All women suffer from a suppressed revolt against the inhibitions forced upon them by our artificial culture, and this suppressed revolt, by well known Freudian means, produces a complex of mental symptoms that is familiar to all of us. At one end of the scale we observe the suffragette, with her grotesque adoption of the male belief in laws, phrases and talismans, and her hysterical demand for a sexual libertarianism that she could not put to use if she had it. And at the other end we find the snuffling and neurotic woman, with her bogus martyrdom, her extravagant pruderies and her pathological delusions. As Ibsen observed long ago, this is a man's world. Women have broken many of their old chains, but they are still enmeshed in a formidable network of man-made taboos and sentimentalities, and it will take them another generation, at least, to get genuine freedom. That this is true is shown by the deep unrest that yet marks the sex, despite its recent progress toward social, political and economic equality. It is almost impossible to find a man who honestly wishes that he were a woman, but almost every woman, at some time or other in her life, is gnawed by a regret that she is not a man.

Two of the hardest things that women have to bear are (a) the stupid masculine disinclination to admit their intellectual superiority, or even their equality, or even their possession of a normal human equipment for thought, and (b) the equally stupid masculine doctrine that they constitute a special and ineffable species of vertebrate, without the natural instincts and appetites of the order—to adapt a phrase from Hackle, that they are transcendental and almost gaseous mammals, and marked by a complete lack of certain salient mammalian characters. The first imbecility has already concerned us at length. One finds traces of it even in works professedly devoted to disposing of it. In one such book, for example, I come upon this: "What all the skill and constructive capacity of the physicians in the Crimean War failed to accomplish Florence Nightingale accomplished by her beautiful femininity and nobility of soul." In other words, by her possession of some recondite and indescribable magic, sharply separated from the ordinary mental processes of man. The theory is unsound and preposterous. Miss Nightingale accomplished her useful work, not by magic, but by hard common sense. The problem before her was simply one of organization. Many men had tackled it, and all of them had failed stupendously. What she did was to bring her feminine sharpness of wit, her feminine clear-thinking, to bear upon it. Thus attacked, it yielded quickly, and once it had been brought to order it was easy for other persons to carry on what she had begun. But the opinion of a man's world still prefers to credit her success to some mysterious angelical quality, unstatable in lucid terms and having no more reality than the divine inspiration of an archbishop. Her extraordinarily acute and accurate intelligence is thus conveniently put upon the table, and the amour propre of man is kept inviolate. To confess frankly that she had more sense than any male Englishman of her generation would be to utter a truth too harsh to be bearable.

The second delusion commonly shows itself in the theory, already discussed, that women are devoid of any sex instinct—that they submit to the odious caresses of the lubricious male only by a powerful effort of the will, and with the sole object of discharging their duty to posterity. It would be impossible to go into this delusion with proper candour and at due length in a work designed for reading aloud in the domestic circle; all I can do is to refer the student to the books of any competent authority on the psychology of sex, say Ellis, or to the confidences (if they are obtainable) of any complaisant bachelor of his acquaintance.

39.

Women as Christians

The glad tidings preached by Christ were obviously highly favourable to women. He lifted them to equality before the Lord when their very possession of souls was still doubted by the majority of rival theologians. Moreover, He esteemed them socially and set value upon their sagacity, and one of the most disdained of their sex, a lady formerly in public life, was among His regular advisers. Mariolatry is thus by no means the invention of the mediaeval popes, as Protestant theologians would have us believe. On the contrary, it is plainly discernible in the Four

Gospels. What the mediaeval popes actually invented (or, to be precise, reinvented, for they simply borrowed the elements of it from St. Paul) was the doctrine of women's inferiority, the precise opposite of the thing credited to them. Committed, for sound reasons of discipline, to the celibacy of the clergy, they had to support it by depicting all traffic with women in the light of a hazardous and ignominious business. The result was the deliberate organization and development of the theory of female triviality, lack of responsibility and general looseness of mind. Woman became a sort of devil, but without the admired intelligence of the regular demons. The appearance of women saints, however, offered a constant and embarrassing criticism of this idiotic doctrine. If occasional women were fit to sit upon the right hand of God—and they were often proving it, and forcing the church to acknowledge it—then surely all women could not be as bad as the books made them out. There thus arose the concept of the angelic woman, the natural vestal; we see her at full length in the romances of mediaeval chivalry. What emerged in the end was a sort of double doctrine, first that women were devils and secondly that they were angels. This preposterous dualism has merged, as we have seen, into a compromise dogma in modern times. By that dogma it is held, on the one hand, that women are unintelligent and immoral, and on the other hand, that they are free from all those weaknesses of the flesh which distinguish men. This, roughly speaking, is the notion of the average male numskull today.

Christianity has thus both libelled women and flattered them, but with the weight always on the side of the libel. It is therefore at bottom, their enemy, as the religion of Christ, now wholly extinct, was their friend. And as they gradually throw off the shackles that have bound them for a thousand years they show appreciation of the fact. Women, indeed, are not naturally religious, and they are growing less and less religious as year chases year. Their ordinary devotion has little if any pious exaltation in it; it is a routine practice, force on them by the masculine notion that an appearance of holiness is proper to their lowly station, and a masculine feeling that church-going somehow keeps them in order, and out of doings that would be less reassuring. When they exhibit any genuine religious fervour, its sexual character is usually so obvious that even the majority of men are cognizant of it. Women never go flocking ecstatically to a church in which the agent of God in the pulpit is an elderly asthmatic with a watchful wife. When one finds them driven to frenzies by the merits of the saints, and weeping over the sorrows of the heathen, and rushing out to haul the whole vicinage up to grace, and spending hours on their knees in hysterical abasement before the heavenly throne, it is quite safe to assume, even without an actual visit, that the ecclesiastic who has worked the miracle is a fair and toothsome fellow, and a good deal more aphrodisiacal than learned. All the great preachers to women in modern times have been men of suave and ingratiating habit, and the great majority of them, from Henry Ward Beecher up and down, have been taken, soon or late, in transactions far more suitable to the boudoir than to the footstool of the Almighty. Their famous killings have always been made among the silliest sort of women—the sort, in brief, who fall so short of the normal acumen of their sex that they are bemused by mere beauty in men.

Such women are in a minority, and so the sex shows a good deal fewer religious enthusiasts per mille than the sex of sentiment and belief. Attending, several years ago, the gladiatorial shows of the Rev. Dr. Billy Sunday, the celebrated American pulpit-clown, I was constantly struck by the great preponderance of males in the pen devoted to the saved. Men of all ages and in enormous numbers came swarming to the altar, loudly bawling for help against their sins, but the women were anything but numerous, and the few who appeared were chiefly either chlorotic adolescents or pathetic old Saufschwestern. For six nights running I sat directly beneath the gifted exhorter without seeing a single female convert of what statisticians call the child-bearing age—that is, the age of maximum intelligence and charm. Among the male simpletons bagged by his yells during this time were the president of a railroad, half a dozen rich bankers and merchants, and the former governor of an American state. But not a woman of comparable position or dignity. Not a woman that any self-respecting bachelor would care to chuck under the chin.

This cynical view of religious emotionalism, and with it of the whole stock of ecclesiastical balderdash, is probably responsible, at least in part, for the reluctance of women to enter upon the sacerdotal career. In those Christian sects which still bar them from the pulpit—usually on the imperfectly concealed ground that they are not equal to its alleged demands upon the morals and the intellect—one never hears of them protesting against the prohibition; they are quite content to leave the degrading imposture to men, who are better fitted for it by talent and conscience. And in those baroque sects, chiefly American, which admit them they show no eagerness to put on the stole and chasuble. When the first clergywoman appeared in the United States, it was predicted by alarmists that men would be driven out of the pulpit by the new competition. Nothing of the sort has occurred, nor is it in prospect. The whole corps of female divines in the country might be herded into one small room. Women, when literate at all, are far too intelligent to make effective ecclesiastics. Their sharp sense of reality is in endless opposition to the whole sacerdotal masquerade, and their cynical humour stands against the snorting that is inseparable from pulpit oratory.

Those women who enter upon the religious life are almost invariably moved by some motive distinct from mere pious inflammation. It is a commonplace, indeed, that, in Catholic countries, girls are driven into convents by economic considerations or by disasters of amour far oftener than they are drawn there by the hope of heaven. Read the lives of the female saints, and you will see how many of them tried marriage and failed at it before ever they turned to religion. In Protestant lands very few women adopt it as a profession at all, and among the few a secular impulse is almost always visible. The girl who is suddenly overcome by a desire to minister to the heathen in foreign lands is nearly invariably found, on inspection, to be a girl harbouring a theory that it would be agreeable to marry some heroic missionary. In point of fact, she duly marries him. At home, perhaps, she has found it impossible to get a husband, but in the remoter marches of China, Senegal and Somaliland, with no white competition present, it is equally impossible to fail.

40.

Piety as a Social Habit

What remains of the alleged piety of women is little more than a social habit, reinforced in most communities by a paucity of other and more inviting divertissements. If you have ever observed the women of Spain and Italy at their devotions you need not be told how much the worship of God may be a mere excuse for relaxation and gossip. These women, in their daily lives, are surrounded by a formidable network of mediaeval taboos; their normal human desire for ease and freedom in intercourse is opposed by masculine distrust and superstition; they meet no strangers; they see and hear nothing new. In the house of the Most High they escape from that vexing routine. Here they may brush shoulders with a crowd. Here, so to speak, they may crane their mental necks and stretch their spiritual legs. Here, above all, they may come into some sort of contact with men relatively more affable, cultured and charming than their husbands and fathers—to wit, with the rev. clergy.

Elsewhere in Christendom, though women are not quite so relentlessly watched and penned up, they feel much the same need of variety and excitement, and both are likewise on tap in the temples of the Lord. No one, I am sure, need be told that the average missionary society or church sewing circle is not primarily a religious organization. Its actual purpose is precisely that of the absurd clubs and secret orders to which the lower and least resourceful classes of men belong: it offers a means of refreshment, of self-expression, of personal display, of political manipulation and boasting, and, if the pastor happens to be interesting, of discreet and almost lawful intrigue. In the course of a life largely devoted to the study of pietistic phenomena, I have never met a single woman who cared an authentic damn for the actual heathen. The attraction in their salvation is always almost purely social. Women go to church for the same reason that farmers and convicts go to church.

Finally, there is the aesthetic lure. Religion, in most parts of Christendom, holds out the only bait of beauty that the inhabitants are ever cognizant of. It offers music, dim lights, relatively ambitious architecture, eloquence, formality and mystery, the caressing meaninglessness that is at the heart of poetry. Women are far more responsive to such things than men, who are ordinarily quite as devoid of aesthetic sensitiveness as so many oxen. The attitude of the typical man toward beauty in its various forms is, in fact, an attitude of suspicion and hostility. He does not regard a work of art as merely inert and stupid; he regards it as, in some indefinable way, positively offensive. He sees the artist as a professional voluptuary and scoundrel, and would no more trust him in his household than he would trust a coloured clergyman in his hen-yard. It was men, and not women, who invented such sordid and literal faiths as those of the Mennonites, Dunkards, Wesleyans and Scotch Presbyterians, with their antipathy to beautiful ritual, their obscene buttonholing of God, their great talent for reducing the ineffable mystery of religion to a mere bawling of idiots. The normal woman, in so far as she has any religion at all, moves irresistibly toward Catholicism, with its poetical obscurantism. The evangelical Protestant sects have a hard time holding her. She can no more be an actual Methodist than a gentleman can be a Methodist.

This inclination toward beauty, of course, is dismissed by the average male blockhead as no more than a feeble sentimentality. The truth is that it is precisely the opposite. It is surely not sentimentality to be moved by the stately and mysterious ceremony of the mass, or even, say, by those timid imitations of it which one observes in certain Protestant churches. Such proceedings, whatever their defects from the standpoint of a pure aesthetic, are at all events vastly more beautiful than any of the private acts of the folk who take part in them. They lift themselves above the barren utilitarianism of everyday life, and no less above the maudlin sentimentalities that men seek pleasure in. They offer a means of escape, convenient and inviting, from that sordid routine of thought and occupation which women revolt against so pertinaciously.

41.

The Ethics of Women

I have said that the religion preached by Jesus (now wholly extinct in the world) was highly favourable to women. This was not saying, of course, that women have repaid the compliment by adopting it. They are, in fact, indifferent Christians in the primitive sense, just as they are bad Christians in the antagonistic modern sense, and particularly on the side of ethics. If they actually accept the renunciations commanded by the Sermon on the Mount, it is only in an effort to flout their substance under cover of their appearance. No woman is really humble; she is merely politic. No woman, with a free choice before her, chooses self-immolation; the most she genuinely desires in that direction is a spectacular martyrdom. No woman delights in poverty. No woman yields when she can prevail. No woman is honestly meek.

In their practical ethics, indeed, women pay little heed to the precepts of the Founder of Christianity, and the fact has passed into proverb. Their gentleness, like the so-called honour of men, is visible only in situations which offer them no menace. The moment a woman finds herself confronted by an antagonist genuinely dangerous, either to her own security or to the well-being of those under her protection—say a child or a husband—she displays a bellicosity which stops at nothing, however outrageous. In the courts of law one occasionally encounters a male extremist who tells the truth, the whole truth and nothing but the truth, even when it is against his cause, but no such woman has ever been on view since the days of Justinian. It is, indeed, an axiom of the bar that women invariably lie upon the stand, and the whole effort of a barrister who has one for a client is devoted to keeping her within bounds, that the obtuse suspicions of the male jury may not be unduly aroused. Women litigants almost always win their cases, not, as is commonly assumed, because the jurymen fall in love with them, but simply and solely because they are clear-headed, resourceful, implacable and without qualms.

What is here visible in the halls of justice, in the face of a vast technical equipment for combating mendacity, is ten times more obvious in freer fields. Any man who is so unfortunate as to have a serious controversy with a woman, say in the departments of finance, theology or amour, must inevitably carry away from it a sense of having passed through a dangerous and almost gruesome experience. Women not only bite in the clinches; they bite even in open fighting; they have a dental reach, so to speak, of amazing length. No attack is so desperate that they will not undertake it, once they are aroused; no device is so unfair and horrifying that it stays them. In my early days, desiring to improve my prose, I served for a year or so as reporter for a newspaper in a police court, and during that time I heard perhaps four hundred cases of so-called wife-beating. The husbands, in their defence, almost invariably pleaded justification, and some of them told such tales of studied atrocity at the domestic hearth, both psychic and physical, that the learned magistrate discharged them with tears in his eyes and the very catchpolls in the courtroom had to blow their noses. Many more men than women go insane, and many more married men than single men. The fact puzzles no one who has had the same opportunity that I had to find out what goes on, year in and year out, behind the doors of apparently happy homes. A woman, if she hates her husband (and many of them do), can make life so sour and obnoxious to him that even death upon the gallows seems sweet by comparison. This hatred, of course, is often, and perhaps Almost invariably, quite justified. To be the wife of an ordinary man, indeed, is an experience that must be very hard to bear. The hollowness and vanity of the fellow, his petty meanness and stupidity, his puling sentimentality and credulity, his bombastic air of a cock on a dunghill, his anaesthesia to all whispers and summonings of the spirit, above all, his loathsome clumsiness in amour—all these things must revolt any woman above the lowest. To be the object of the oafish affections of such a creature, even when they are honest and profound, cannot be expected to give any genuine joy to a woman of sense and refinement. His performance as a gallant, as Honor de Balzac long ago observed, unescapably suggests a gorilla's efforts to play the violin. Women survive the tragicomedy only by dint of their great capacity for play-acting. They are able to act so realistically that often they deceive even themselves; the average woman's contentment, indeed, is no more than a tribute to her histrionism. But there must be innumerable revolts in secret, even so, and one sometimes wonders that so few women, with the thing so facile and so safe, poison their husbands. Perhaps it is not quite as rare as vital statistics make it out; the deathrate among husbands is very much higher than among wives. More than once, indeed, I have gone to the funeral of an acquaintance who died suddenly, and observed a curious glitter in the eyes of the inconsolable widow.

Even in this age of emancipation, normal women have few serious transactions in life save with their husbands and potential husbands; the business of marriage is their dominant concern from adolescence to senility. When they step outside their habitual circle they show the same alert and eager wariness that they exhibit within it. A man who has dealings with them must keep his wits about him, and even when he is most cautious he is often flabbergasted by their sudden and unconscionable forays. Whenever woman goes into trade she quickly gets a reputation as a sharp trader. Every little town in America has its Hetty Green, each sweating blood from turnips, each the terror of all the male usurers of the neighbourhood. The man who tackles such an amazon of barter takes his fortune into his hands; he has little more chance of success against the feminine technique in business than he has against the feminine technique in marriage. In both arenas the advantage of women lies in their freedom from sentimentality. In business they address themselves wholly to their own profit, and give no thought whatever to the hopes, aspirations and amour propre of their antagonists. And in the duel of sex they fence, not to make points, but to disable and disarm. Aman, when he succeeds in throwing off a woman who has attempted to marry him, always carries away a maudlin sympathy for her in her defeat and dismay. But no one ever heard of a woman who pitied the poor fellow whose honest passion she had found it expedient to spurn. On the contrary, women take delight in such clownish agonies, and exhibit them proudly, and boast about them to other women.

V

The New Age

42.

The Transvaluation of Values

The gradual emancipation of women that has been going on for the last century has still a long way to proceed before they are wholly delivered from their traditional burdens and so stand clear of the oppressions of men. But already, it must be plain, they have made enormous progress—perhaps more than they made in the ten thousand years preceding. The rise of the industrial system, which has borne so harshly upon the race in general, has brought them certain unmistakable benefits. Their economic dependence, though still sufficient to make marriage highly attractive to them, is nevertheless so far broken down that large classes of women are now almost free agents, and quite independent of the favour of men. Most of these women, responding to ideas that are still powerful, are yet intrigued, of course, by marriage, and prefer it to the autonomy that is coming in, but the fact remains that they now have a free choice in the matter, and that dire necessity no longer controls them. After all, they needn't marry if they don't want to; it is possible to get their bread by their own labour in the workshops of the world. Their grandmothers were in a far more difficult position. Failing marriage, they not only suffered a cruel ignominy, but in many cases faced the menace of actual starvation. There was simply no respectable place in the economy of those times for the free woman. She either had to enter a nunnery or accept a disdainful patronage that was as galling as charity.

Nothing could be, plainer than the effect that the increasing economic security of women is having upon their whole habit of life and mind. The diminishing marriage rate and the even more rapidly diminishing birth rates how which way the wind is blowing. It is common for male statisticians, with characteristic imbecility, to ascribe the fall in the marriage rate to a growing disinclination on the male side. This growing disinclination is actually on the female side. Even though no considerable, body of women has yet reached the definite doctrine that marriage is less desirable than freedom, it must be plain that large numbers of them now approach the business with far greater fastidiousness than their grandmothers or even their mothers exhibited. They are harder to please, and hence pleased less often. The woman of a century ago could imagine nothing more favourable to her than marriage; even marriage with a fifth rate man was better than no marriage at all. This notion is gradually feeling the opposition of a contrary notion. Women in general may still prefer marriage, to work, but there is an increasing minority which begins to realize that work may offer the greater contentment, particularly if it be mellowed by a certain amount of philandering.

There already appears in the world, indeed, a class of women, who, while still not genuinely averse to marriage, are yet free from any theory that it is necessary, or even invariably desirable. Among these women are a goodman somewhat vociferous propagandists, almost male in their violent earnestness; they range from the man eating suffragettes to such preachers of free motherhood as Ellen Key and such professional shockers of the bourgeoisie as the American prophetess of birth-control, Margaret Sanger. But among them are many more who wake the world with no such noisy eloquence, but content themselves with carrying out their ideas in a quiet and respectable manner. The number of such women is much larger than is generally imagined, and that number tends to increase steadily. They are women who, with their economic independence assured, either by inheritance or by their own efforts, chiefly in the arts and professions, do exactly as they please, and make no pother about it. Naturally enough, their superiority to convention and the common frenzy makes them extremely attractive to the better sort of men, and so it is not uncommon for one of them to find herself voluntarily sought in marriage, without any preliminary scheming by herself—surely an experience that very few ordinary women ever enjoy, save perhaps in dreams or delirium.

The old order changeth and giveth place to the new. Among the women's clubs and in the women's colleges, I have no doubt, there is still much debate of the old and silly question: Are platonic relations possible between the sexes? In other words, is friendship possible without sex? Many a woman of the new order dismisses the problem with another question: Why without sex? With the decay of the ancient concept of women as property there must come inevitably a reconsideration of the whole sex question, and out of that reconsideration there must come a revision of the mediaeval penalties which now punish the slightest frivolity in the female. The notion that honour in women is exclusively a physical matter, that a single aberrance may convert a woman of the highest merits into a woman of none at all, that the sole valuable thing a woman can bring to marriage is virginity—this notion is so preposterous that no intelligent person, male or female, actually cherishes it. It survives as one of the hollow conventions of Christianity; nay, of the levantine barbarism that preceded Christianity. As women throw off the other conventions which now bind them they will throw off this one, too, and so their virtue, grounded upon fastidiousness and self-respect instead of upon mere fear and conformity, will become afar more laudable thing than it ever can be under the present system. And for its absence, if they see fit to dispose of it, they will no more apologize. than a man apologizes today.

43.

The Lady of Joy

Even prostitution, in the long run, may become a more or less respectable profession, as it was in the great days of the Greeks. That quality will surely attach to it if ever it grows quite unnecessary; whatever is unnecessary is always respectable, for example, religion, fashionable clothing, and a knowledge of Latin grammar. The prostitute is disesteemed today, not because her trade involves anything intrinsically degrading or even disagreeable, but because she is currently assumed to have been driven into it by dire necessity, against her dignity and inclination. That this assumption is usually unsound is no objection to it; nearly all the thinking of the world, particularly in the field of morals, is based upon unsound assumption, e.g., that God observes the fall of a sparrow and is shocked by the fall of a Sunday-school superintendent. The truth is that prostitution is one of the most attractive of the occupations practically open to the sort of women who engage in it, and that the prostitute commonly likes her work, and would not exchange places with a shop-girl or a waitress for anything in the world. The notion to the contrary is propagated by unsuccessful prostitutes who fall into the hands of professional reformers, and who assent to the imbecile theories of the latter in order to cultivate their good will, just as convicts in prison, questioned by tee-totalers, always ascribe their rascality to alcohol. No prostitute of anything resembling normal intelligence is under the slightest duress; she is perfectly free to abandon her trade and go into a shop or factory or into domestic service whenever the impulse strikes her; all the prevailing gabble about white slave jails and kidnappers comes from pious rogues who make a living by feeding such nonsense to the credulous. So long as the average prostitute is able to make a good living, she is quite content with her lot, and disposed to contrast it egotistically with the slavery of her virtuous sisters. If she complains of it, then you may be sure that her success is below her expectations. A starving lawyer always sees injustice, in the courts. A bad physician is a bitter critic of Ehrlich and Pasteur. And when a suburban clergyman is forced out of his cure by a vestry-room revolution be almost invariably concludes that the sinfulness of man is incurable, and sometimes he even begins to doubt some of the typographical errors in Holy Writ.

The high value set upon virginity by men, whose esteem of it is based upon a mixture of vanity and voluptuousness, causes many women to guard it in their own persons with a jealousy far beyond their private inclinations and interests. It is their theory that the loss of it would materially impair their chances of marriage. This theory is not supported by the facts. The truth is that the woman who sacrifices her chastity, everything else being equal, stands a much better chance of making a creditable marriage than the woman who remains chaste. This is especially true of women of the lower economic classes. At once they come into contact, hitherto socially difficult and sometimes almost impossible, with men of higher classes, and begin to take on, with the curious facility of their sex, the refinements and tastes and points of view of those classes. The mistress thus gathers charm, and what has begun as a sordid sale of amiability not uncommonly ends with formal marriage. The number of such marriages is enormously greater than appears superficially, for both parties obviously make every effort to conceal the facts. Within the circle of my necessarily limited personal acquaintance I know of scores of men, some of them of wealth and position, who have made such marriages, and who do not seem to regret it. It is an old observation, indeed, that a woman who has previously dispose of her virtue makes a good wife. The common theory is that this is because she is grateful to her husband for rescuing her from social outlawry; the truth is that she makes a good wife because she is a shrewd woman, and has specialized professionally in masculine weakness, and is thus extra-competent at the traditional business of her sex. Such a woman often shows a truly magnificent sagacity. It is very difficult to deceive her logically, and it is impossible to disarm her emotionally. Her revolt against the pruderies and sentimentalities of the world was evidence, to begin with, of her intellectual enterprise and courage, and her success as a rebel is proof of her extraordinary pertinacity, resourcefulness and acumen.

Even the most lowly prostitute is better off, in all worldly ways, than the virtuous woman of her own station in life. She has less work to do, it is less monotonous and dispiriting, she meets a far greater variety of men, and they are of classes distinctly beyond her own. Nor is her occupation hazardous and her ultimate fate tragic. A dozen or more years ago I observed a some what amusing proof of this last. At that time certain sentimental busybodies of the American city in which I lived undertook an elaborate inquiry into prostitution therein, and some of them came to me in advance, as a practical journalist, for advice as to how to proceed. I found that all of them shared the common superstition that the professional life of the average prostitute is only five years long, and that she invariably ends in the gutter. They were enormously amazed When they unearthed the truth. This truth was to the effect that the average prostitute of that town ended her career, not in the morgue but at the altar of God, and that those who remained unmarried often continued in practice for ten, fifteen and even twenty years, and then retired on competences. It was established, indeed, that fully eighty per cent married, and that they almost always got husbands who would have been far beyond their reach had they remained virtuous. For one who married a cabman or petty pugilist there were a dozen who married respectable mechanics, policemen, small shopkeepers and minor officials, and at least two or three who married well-to-do tradesmen and professional men. Among the thousands whose careers were studied there was actually one who ended as the wife of the town's richest banker—that is, one who bagged the best catch in the whole community. This woman had begun as a domestic servant, and abandoned that harsh and dreary life to enter a brothel. Her experiences there polished and civilized her, and in her old age she was a grande dame of great dignity. Much of the sympathy wasted upon women of the ancient profession is grounded upon an error as to their own attitude toward it. An educated woman, hearing that a frail sister in a public stew is expected to be amiable to all sorts of bounders, thinks of how she would shrink from such contacts, and so concludes that the actual prostitute suffers acutely. What she overlooks is that these men, however gross and repulsive they may appear to her, are measurably superior to men of the prostitute's own class—say her father and brothers—and that communion with them, far from being disgusting, is often rather romantic. I well remember observing, during my collaboration with the vice-crusaders aforesaid, the delight of a lady of joy who had attracted the notice of a police lieutenant; she was intensely pleased by the idea of having a client of such haughty manners, such brilliant dress, and what seemed to her to be so dignified a profession. It is always forgotten that this weakness is not confined to prostitutes, but run through the whole female sex. The woman who could not imagine an illicit affair with a wealthy soap manufacturer or even with a lawyer finds it quite easy to imagine herself succumbing to an ambassador or a duke. There are very few exceptions to this rule. In the most reserved of modern societies the women who represent their highest flower are notoriously complaisant to royalty. And royal women, to complete the circuit, not infrequently yield to actors and musicians, i.e., to men radiating a glamour not encountered even in princes.

44.

The Future of Marriage

The transvaluation of values that is now in progress will go on slowly and for a very long while. That it will ever be quite complete is, of course, impossible. There are inherent differences will continue to show themselves until the end of time. As woman gradually becomes convinced, not only of the possibility of economic independence, but also of its value, she will probably lose her present overmastering desire for marriage, and address herself to meeting men in free economic competition. That is to say, she will address herself to acquiring that practical competence, that high talent for puerile and chiefly mechanical expertness, which now sets man ahead of her in the labour market of the world. To do this she will have to sacrifice some of her present intelligence; it is impossible to imagine a genuinely intelligent human being becoming a competent trial lawyer, or buttonhole worker, or newspaper sub-editor, or piano tuner, or house painter. Women, to get upon all fours with men in such stupid occupations, will have to commit spiritual suicide, which is probably much further than they will ever actually go. Thus a shade of their present superiority to men will always remain, and with it a shade of their relative inefficiency, and so marriage will remain attractive to them, or at all events to most of them, and its overthrow will be prevented. To abolish it entirely, as certain fevered reformers propose, would be as difficult as to abolish the precession of the equinoxes.

At the present time women vacillate somewhat absurdly between two schemes of life, the old and the new. On the one hand, their economic independence is still full of conditions, and on the other hand they are in revolt against the immemorial conventions. The result is a general unrest, with many symptoms of extravagant and unintelligent revolt. One of those symptoms is the appearance of intellectual striving in women—not a striving, alas, toward the genuine pearls and rubies of the mind, but one merely toward the acquirement of the rubber stamps that men employ in their so-called thinking. Thus we have women who launch themselves into party politics, and fill their heads with a vast mass of useless knowledge about political tricks, customs, theories and personalities. Thus, too, we have the woman social reformer, trailing along ridiculously behind a tatterdemalion posse of male utopians, each with something to sell. And thus we have the woman who goes in for advanced wisdom of the sort on draught in women's clubs—in brief, the sort of wisdom which consists entirely of a body of beliefs and propositions that are ignorant, unimportant and untrue. Such banal striving is most prodigally on display in the United States, where superficiality amounts to a national disease. Its popularity is due to the relatively greater leisure of the American people, who work less than any other people in the world, and, above all, to the relatively greater leisure of American women. Thousands of them have been emancipated from any compulsion to productive labour without having acquired any compensatory intellectual or artistic interest or social duty. The result is that they swarm in the women's clubs, and waste their time, listening to bad poetry, worse music, and still worse lectures on Maeterlinck, Balkan politics and the subconscious. It is among such women that one observes the periodic rages for Bergsonism, the Montessori method, the twilight sleep and other such follies, so pathetically characteristic of American culture.

One of the evil effects of this tendency I have hitherto descanted upon, to wit, the growing disposition of American women to regard all routine labour, particularly in the home, as infra dignitatem and hence intolerable. Out of' that notion arise many lamentable phenomena. On the one hand, we have the spectacle of a great number of healthy and well-fed women engage in public activities that, nine times out of ten, are meaningless, mischievous and a nuisance, and on the other hand we behold such a decay in the domestic arts that, at the first onslaught of the late war, the national government had to import a foreign expert to teach the housewives of the country the veriest elements of thrift. No such instruction was needed by the housewives of the Continent. They were simply told how much food they could have, and their natural competence did the rest. There is never any avoidable waste there, either in peace or in war. A French housewife has little use for a garbage can, save as a depository for uplifting literature. She does her best with the means at her disposal, not only in war time but at all times.

As I have said over and over again in this inquiry, a woman's disinclination to acquire the intricate expertness that lies at the bottom of good housekeeping is due primarily to her active intelligence; it is difficult for her to concentrate her mind upon such stupid and meticulous enterprises. But whether difficult or easy, it is obviously important for the average woman to make some effort in that direction, for if she fails to do so there is chaos. That chaos is duly visible in the United States. Here women reveal one of their subterranean qualities: their deficiency in conscientiousness. They are quite without that dog-like fidelity to duty which is one of the shining marks of men. They never summon up a high pride in doing what is inherently disagreeable; they always go to the galleys under protest, and with vows of sabotage; their fundamental philosophy is almost that of the syndicalists. The sentimentality of men connives at this, and is thus largely responsible for it. Before the average puella, apprenticed in the kitchen, can pick up a fourth of the culinary subtleties that are commonplace even to the chefs on dining cars, she has caught aman and need concern herself about them no more, for he has to eat, in the last analysis, whatever she sets before him, and his lack of intelligence makes it easy for her to shut off his academic criticisms by bald appeals to his emotions. By an easy process he finally attaches a positive value to her indolence. It is a proof, he concludes, of her fineness of soul. In the presence of her lofty incompetence he is abashed.

But as women, gaining economic autonomy, meet men in progressively bitterer competition, the rising masculine distrust and fear of them will be reflected even in the enchanted domain of marriage, and the husband, having yielded up most of his old rights, will begin to reveal anew jealousy of those that remain, and particularly of the right to a fair quid pro quo for his own docile industry. In brief, as women shake off their ancient disabilities they will also shake off some of their ancient immunities, and their doings will come to be regarded with a soberer and more exigent scrutiny than now prevails. The extension of the suffrage, I believe, will encourage this awakening; in wresting it from the reluctant male the women of the western world have planted dragons' teeth, the which will presently leap up and gnaw them. Now that women have the political power to obtain their just rights, they will begin to lose their old power to obtain special privileges by sentimental appeals. Men, facing them squarely, will consider them anew, not as romantic political and social invalids, to be coddled and caressed, but as free competitors in a harsh world. When that reconsideration gets under way there will be a general overhauling of the relations between the sexes, and some of the fair ones, I suspect, will begin to wonder why they didn't let well enough alone.

45.

Effects of the War

The present series of wars, it seems likely, will continue for twenty or thirty years, and perhaps longer. That the first clash was inconclusive was shown brilliantly by the preposterous nature of the peace finally reached—a peace so artificial and dishonest that the signing of it was almost equivalent to anew declaration of war. At least three new contests in the grand manner are plainly insight—one between Germany and France to rectify the unnatural tyranny of a weak and incompetent nation over a strong and enterprising nation, one between Japan and the United States for the mastery of the Pacific, and one between England and the United States for the control of the sea. To these must be added various minor struggles, and perhaps one or two of almost major character: the effort of Russia to regain her old unity and power, the effort of the Turks to put down the slave rebellion (of Greeks, Armenians, Arabs, etc.)which now menaces them, the effort of the Latin-Americans to throw off the galling Yankee yoke, and the joint effort of Russia and Germany (perhaps with England and Italy aiding) to get rid of such international nuisances as the insane polish republic, the petty states of the Baltic, and perhaps also most of the Balkan states. I pass over the probability of a new mutiny in India, of the rising of China against the Japanese, and of a general struggle for a new alignment of boundaries in

South America. All of these wars, great and small, are probable; most of them are humanly certain. They will be fought ferociously, and with the aid of destructive engines of the utmost efficiency. They will bring about an unparalleled butchery of men, and a large proportion of these men will be under forty years of age.

As a result there will be a shortage of husbands in Christendom, and as a second result the survivors will be appreciably harder to snare than the men of today. Every man of agreeable exterior and easy means will be pursued, not merely by a few dozen or score of women, as now, but by whole battalions and brigades of them, and he will be driven in sheer self-defence into very sharp bargaining. Perhaps in the end the state will have to interfere in the business, to prevent the potential husband going to waste in the turmoil of opportunity.

Just what form this interference is likely to take has not yet appeared clearly. In France there is already a wholesale legitimization of children born out of wedlock and in Eastern Europe there has been a clamour for the legalization of polygamy, but these devices do not meet the main problem, which is the encouragement of monogamy to the utmost. A plan that suggests itself is the amelioration of the position of the monogamous husband, now rendered increasingly uncomfortable by the laws of most Christian states. I do not think that the more intelligent sort of women, faced by a perilous shortage of men, would object seriously to that amelioration. They must see plainly that the present system, if it is carried much further, will begin to work powerfully against their best interests, if only by greatly reinforcing the disinclination to marriage that already exists among the better sort of men. The woman of true discretion, I am convinced, would much rather marry a superior man, even on unfavourable terms, than make John Smith her husband, serf and prisoner at one stroke.

The law must eventually recognize this fact and make provision for it. The average husband, perhaps, deserves little succour. The woman who pursues and marries him, though she may be moved by selfish aims, should be properly rewarded by the state for her service to it—a service surely not to be lightly estimated in a military age. And that reward may conveniently take the form, as in the United States, of statutes giving her title to a large share of his real property and requiring him to surrender most of his income to her, and releasing her from all obedience to him and from all obligation to keep his house in order. But the woman who aspires to higher game should be quite willing, it seems to me, to resign some of these advantages in compensation for the greater honour and satisfaction of being wife to a man of merit, and mother to his children. All that is needed is laws allowing her, if she will, to resign her right of dower, her right to maintenance and her immunity from discipline, and to make any other terms that she may be led to regard as equitable. At present women are unable to make most of these concessions even if they would: the laws of the majority of western nations are inflexible. If, for example, an Englishwoman should agree, by an ante-nuptial contract, to submit herself to the discipline, not of the current statutes, but of the elder common law, which allowed a husband to correct his wife corporally with a stick no thicker than his thumb, it would be competent for any sentimental neighbour to set the agreement at naught by haling her husband before a magistrate for carrying it out, and it is a safe wager that the magistrate would jail him.

This plan, however novel it may seem, is actually already in operation. Many a married woman, in order to keep her husband from revolt, makes more or less disguised surrenders of certain of the rights and immunities that she has under existing laws. There are, for example, even in America, women who practise the domestic arts with competence and diligence, despite the plain fact that no legal penalty would be visited upon them if they failed to do so. There are women who follow external trades and professions, contributing a share to the family exchequer. There are women who obey their husbands, even against their best judgments. There are, most numerous of all, women who wink discreetly at husbandly departures, overt or in mere intent, from the oath of chemical purity taken at the altar. It is a commonplace, indeed, that many happy marriages admit a party of the third part. There would be more of them if there were more women with enough serenity of mind to see the practical advantage of the arrangement. The trouble with such triangulations is not primarily that they involve perjury or that they offer any fundamental offence to the wife; if she avoids banal theatricals, in fact, they commonly have the effect of augmenting the husband's devotion to her and respect for her, if only as the fruit of comparison. The trouble with them is that very few men among us have sense enough to manage them intelligently. The masculine mind is readily taken in by specious values; the average married man of Protestant Christendom, if he succumbs at all, succumbs to some meretricious and flamboyant creature, bent only upon fleecing him. Here is where the harsh realism of the Frenchman shows its superiority to the sentimentality of the men of the Teutonic races. A Frenchman would no more think of taking a mistress without consulting his wife than he would think of standing for office without consulting his wife. The result is that he is seldom victimized. For one Frenchman ruined by women there are at least a hundred Englishmen and Americans, despite the fact that a hundred times as many Frenchmen engage in that sort of recreation. The case of Zola is typical. As is well known, his amours were carefully supervised by Mme. Zola from the first days of their marriage, and inconsequence his life was wholly free from scandals and his mind was never distracted from his work.

46.

The Eternal Romance

But whatever the future of monogamous marriage, there will never be any decay of that agreeable adventurousness which now lies at the bottom of all transactions between the sexes. Women may emancipate themselves, they may borrow the whole bag of masculine tricks, and they may cure themselves of their present desire for the vegetable security of marriage, but they will never cease to be women, and so long as they are women they will remain provocative to men. Their chief charm today lies precisely in the fact that they are dangerous, that they threaten masculine liberty and autonomy, that their sharp minds present a menace vastly greater than that of acts of God and the public enemy—and they will be dangerous for ever. Men fear them, and are fascinated by them. They know how to show their teeth charmingly; the more enlightened of them have perfected a superb technique of fascination. It was Nietzsche who called them the recreation of the warrior—not of the poltroon, remember, but of the warrior. A profound saying. They have an infinite capacity for rewarding masculine industry and enterprise with small and irresistible flatteries; their acute understanding combines with their capacity for evoking ideas of beauty to make them incomparable companions when the serious business of the day is done, and the time has come to expand comfortably in the interstellar ether.

Every man, I daresay, has his own notion of what constitutes perfect peace and contentment, but all of those notions, despite the fundamental conflict of the sexes, revolve around women. As for me—and I hope I may be pardoned, at this late stage in my inquiry, for intruding my own personality—I reject the two commonest of them: passion, at least in its more adventurous and melodramatic aspects, is too exciting and alarming for so indolent a man, and I am too egoistic to have much desire to be mothered. What, then, remains for me? Let me try to describe it to you.

It is the close of a busy and vexatious day—say half past five or six o'clock of a winter afternoon. I have had a cocktail or two, and am stretched out on a divan in front of a fire, smoking. At the edge of the divan, close enough for me to reach her with my hand, sits a woman not too young, but still good-looking and well-dressed—above all, a woman with a soft, low-pitched, agreeable voice. As I snooze she talks—of anything, everything, all the things that women talk of: books, music, the play, men, other women. No politics. No business. No religion. No metaphysics. Nothing challenging and vexatious—but remember, she is intelligent; what she says is clearly expressed, and often picturesquely. I observe the fine sheen of her hair, the pretty cut of her frock, the glint of her white teeth, the arch of her eye-brow, the graceful curve of her arm. I listen to the exquisite murmur of her voice. Gradually I fall asleep—but only for an instant. At once, observing it, she raises her voice ever so little, and I am awake. Then to sleep again—slowly and charmingly down that slippery hill of dreams. And then awake again, and then asleep again, and so on.

I ask you seriously: could anything be more unutterably beautiful? The sensation of falling asleep is to me The most exquisite in the world. I delight in it so much that I even look forward to death itself with a sneaking wonder and desire. Well, here is sleep poetized and made doubly sweet. Here is sleep set to the finest music in the world. I match this situation against any that you ran think of. It is not only enchanting; it is also, in a very true sense, ennobling. In the end, when the girl grows prettily miffed and throws me out, I return to my sorrows somehow purged and glorified. I am a better man in my own sight. I have grazed upon the fields of asphodel. I have been genuinely, completely and unregrettably happy.

47.

Apologia in Conclusion

At the end I crave the indulgence of the cultured reader for the imperfections necessarily visible in all that I have here set down—imperfections not only due to incomplete information and fallible logic, but also, and perhaps more importantly, to certain fundamental weaknesses of the sex to which I have the honour to belong. A man is inseparable from his congenital vanities and stupidities, as a dog is inseparable from its fleas. They reveal themselves in everything he says and does, but they reveal themselves most of all when he discusses the majestic mystery of woman. Just as he smirks and rolls his eyes in her actual presence, so he puts on apathetic and unescapable clownishness when he essays to dissect her in the privacy of the laboratory. There is no book on woman by a man that is not a stupendous compendium of posturings and imbecilities. There are but two books that show even a superficial desire to be honest—"The Unexpurgated Case Against Woman Suffrage," by Sir Almroth Wright, and this one. Wright made a gallant attempt to tell the truth, but before he got half way through his task his ineradicable donkeyishness as a male overcame his scientific frenzy as a psychologist, and so he hastily washed his hands of the business, and affronted the judicious with a half baked and preposterous book. Perhaps I have failed too, and even more ingloriously. If so, I am full of sincere and indescribable regret.

BIBLIOBAZAAR

The essential book market!

Did you know that you can get any of our titles in large print?

Did you know that we have an ever-growing collection of books in many languages?

Order online:
www.bibliobazaar.com

Find all of your favorite classic books!

Stay up to date with the latest government reports!

At BiblioBazaar, we aim to make knowledge more accessible by making thousands of titles available to you- *quickly and affordably.*

Contact us:
BiblioBazaar
PO Box 21206
Charleston, SC 29413

Printed in the United Kingdom by
Lightning Source UK Ltd., Milton Keynes
139744UK00001B/57/A